TEEN'S GUIDE
TO MAKING AND SELLING
UPCYCLED
ARTS AND CRAFTS

HOW TO START AND GROW A
REDUCE-REUSE-RECYCLE SIDE GIG

WITHDRAWN

JAMES DILLEHAY

Teen's Guide to Making and Selling Upcycled Arts and Crafts; How to Start and Grow a Reduce-Reuse-Recycle Side Gig

© Copyright 2023 James Dillehay. All rights reserved.

No part of this book may be reproduced in any form without written permission from the publisher. The publisher takes no responsibility for the use of any of the materials or methods described in this book, nor for the products thereof. While all attempts have been made to verify information provided in this publication, neither the author nor the publisher assumes any responsibility for errors, omissions or contrary interpretation of the subject matter herein. This publication is not intended as a substitute for legal or accounting advice. Information contained herein may be subject to different state and/or local laws or regulations.

ISBN: 978-1-7320264-6-9

Warm Snow Publishers
PO Box 170, Torreon, NM 87061

Cover Design by Kostis Pavlou

Publisher's Cataloging-in-Publication Data

Names: Dillehay, James, author.
Title: Teen's guide to making and selling upcycled arts and crafts / James Dillehay.
Description: Torreon, NM : Warm Snow Publishers, 2023. | Summary: Teen's guide to how to upcycle plastic, newspapers, and other trash into art-crafts for consumers. | Audience: Grades 5 & up.
Identifiers: LCCN 2023900738 (print) | 978-1-7320264-6-9 (paperback)
Subjects: LCSH: Gig economy. | Supplementary employment. | CYAC: Recycling (Waste, etc.) | Handicraft. | Sustainability. | Money-making projects. | BISAC: YOUNG ADULT NONFICTION / Recycling & Green Living. | YOUNG ADULT NONFICTION / Crafts & Hobbies. | YOUNG ADULT NONFICTION / Activity Books. | YOUNG ADULT NONFICTION / Activity Books.
Classification: LCC TT149 .D55 2023 (print) | LCC TT149 (ebook) | DDC 680--dc23.

Contents

Introduction 7
   Who is the Book For 8
   What Holds Some Back 8
   What's In This for You 9
   The Opportunity 9
   What's Covered in the Book 10
   What You Need to Start 11
   Why This Book, Why Now 11
   How to Get the Most from the Book 12

CHAPTER 1: Things to Make to Sell **13**
   How to Find Products in Demand 13
   How to Test Market Your Product Idea 17
   How Customers Give You Product Ideas 19
   Making Reproducible Versus One-of-Kind Products ... 19
   Finding Raw Materials 20
   Checklist for Making Products Stand Out 21

Chapter 2: What a Side Hustle Might Look Like **23**
   The Family Side Hustle 24

Chapter 3: Setting Up to Do Business **31**
   Choosing a Name for Your Business 31
   Legal Requirements: Permits and Licenses 32
   Accepting Credit card Payments 33
   Keeping Records / Accounting 34

Chapter 4: Preparing to Market Your Hustle **36**
   Branding Cues 36
   Types of Promotional Materials 38
   Design Resources 40
   Printing Services 41

Chapter 5: How to Price Upcycled Art & Crafts **42**
   Understanding Retail and Wholesale Pricing 42
   How Much Will Shoppers Pay? 43
   What Does It Cost to Make an Item 44
   The Pricing Formula 46
   Your profit margin 47
   Pricing One-Of-a-Kind Items 48
   Lower Your Production Costs 49

Chapter 6: Your Marketing Plan **51**
   101 Marketing-Related Actions.. 51
   Daily Planner / Marketing Calendar 55
Chapter 7: Crowdfunding **57**
Chapter 8: Selling at Art & Craft Shows & Other Events 60
   Types of Events 61
   Be Wary of...62
   Finding Events.. 63
   What Shows Cost..65
   How Much Can You Earn 66
   How to Apply 66
   Displaying Your Products 67
   Checklist for What to Take to Shows 69
   More Tips for Successful Shows...71
Chapter 9: SEO Tips, Search Engine Optimization **74**
   Finding Search Terms Buyers Use..75
   Inbound Links to Your Pages 75
   Engagement 76
   Where to Place Keywords and Tags.................................... 77
   Keyword Tools..79
Chapter 10: Selling On Etsy **81**
   Pre-Setup Steps 82
   Setting Up Your Etsy Shop 82
   Images 84
   Etsy SEO...84
   Product Descriptions...85
   Share on Social Media 86
   Customer Service 86
   Promoted Listings 87
   Market Your Etsy Store Offline..88
   If Sales Are Poor...88
   Get Reviews and Publicity 90
   Etsy Apps 90
   Mailing List... 90
Chapter 11: E-Commerce Alternatives to Etsy...................**91**
   Selling on Amazon Handmade.. 91
   Alternatives to Etsy and Amazon...94
   Setting Up Your Own Domain Site.....................................94
   Online Advertising.. 96
Chapter 12: Blogging... **98**

Chapter 13: Introduction to Social Media..........................100
   Advantages of Social Media...100
   Social Marketing Tips 101
   Social Posts Scheduling Tools 103
   Get Followers on Your Mailing List.................................103
Chapter 14: Facebook Best Practices **104**
Chapter 15: Pinterest Best Practices **108**
Chapter 16: Instagram Best Practices **112**
Chapter 17: TikTok Best Practices **118**
Chapter 18: Selling Wholesale... **121**
   Preparing to Sell Wholesale...121
   Finding Wholesale Buyers 122
   Working with Stores 124
   Overlooked Retailers for Handmade Goods.................126
   Getting Your Recycled Art in Galleries 127
Chapter 19: Upcycled Art in Public Art Programs.............**128**
   Arts councils and arts agencies 128
   Examples of Public Art Programs.....................................129
Chapter 20: Your Customer List... **131**
   Capturing and Working with E-mails.............................131
   Thirty-three Excuses to Follow-up..................................133
   Treat Customers Well...135
Chapter 21: The Success Pattern **136**
Appendix 1: Product Photography **139**
Appendix 2: Find Events **142**
Appendix 3: Where to List Online Around the World.....**144**
Appendix 4: Recycled Art Contests **146**
About the Author **147**
Resources..**148**

Introduction

What if I told you there was money to be made repurposing old newspapers, aluminum cans, glass jars, and other waste destined for landfills?

Teens, young and other adults around the world are transforming upcycling and recycling into thriving, creative side hustles and full-time businesses. You can too, and this book will show you how.

Every side gig or business is built on something people want. Consumers want products that are good for the planet. A study reported on by Forbes showed nearly 90% of consumers around the world say they are concerned about the social and environmental impact of things they buy.

Multiple surveys also reveal shoppers will pay more to own sustainably produced items, according to Fortune.com.

I saw this firsthand when I opened an art and crafts gallery in a popular tourist area near Santa Fe, New Mexico. We got shoppers from all around the world. Pieces made from cleverly repurposed junk attracted more attention and sold for higher prices. Inspired, I designed a scarf from 100% upcycled fibers which outsold all my other models.

Creative upcyclers start their gigs from different motivations. Many want a side hustle to earn extra money. Others want the work they do to make a difference. And some begin from necessity.

After working for Sears for 21 years, Bill Finks lost his job because of a recession. With few work opportunities available, he and his wife, Marcia, began creating art from old tin barn roofs scattered along the countryside. Losing that Sears job may have been a blessing in disguise. Their handmade business grew into a huge success getting mentions in *Country Home, House Beautiful, Country Living, Elle Decor*, and on *Oprah* (see PrimitiveTwig.com).

Who is the Book For

* You are looking for a side hustle that's cheap to start and has a lot of upside potential. You would love a gig that helps the environment.

* You already make and promote handmade products. Your work isn't selling as well as you would like. Going sustainable can give you an edge. Most consumers want businesses they buy from to care about the planet.

* You are retired and need extra income. You would like an easy-to-manage small business you can work on your own schedule.

* You are an entrepreneur who agrees that businesses, large and small, can make a difference and a profit at the same time.

* You are a parent, family member, or teacher looking for ways to create more engagement with young adults. Students around the world are calling on everyone to upcycle and recycle.

What Holds People Back

Starting a creative side hustle is a step-by-step process anyone can do. Even so, many of us encounter roadblocks. Here are common challenges and ways around them.

You think you aren't creative. I thought that, too, before I first learned to make stuff by hand. I believed I could not create anything people would buy. Fortunately, I went ahead and tried it anyway. Some months later, I sold $5,700 at two shows and never looked back.

You don't have a business background. Side gigs don't require previous experience to start. Everything you need to begin is in this guide. It's easier and cheaper than you may think to get set up.

You aren't a salesperson. Welcome to my world! I couldn't sell water to a thirsty man in the desert. My handicap forced me to get good at marketing, which means getting my stuff in front of buyers and letting the work sell itself. I've done very well without ever having to be a salesperson and will show you how.

Plagued by self-doubt? When people buy stuff you have made with your own hands, it builds your self-esteem. If others like me—who started without skills or creative ability—can do it, you can do it, too.

What's In This for You

The book is a blueprint for starting and growing an upcycled art or crafts business. You will love the pay-offs:
- Enjoy extra money.
- Create more freedom.
- Grow your self-confidence.
- Become an example to others by helping make a better world.

How much money can a person earn selling upcycled art or craft products?

The stories throughout this book are from folks making anywhere from a few hundred dollars a month to seven-figures a year. None of the examples guarantee you will get similar results. Your success is literally in your own hands.

The Opportunity

Shoppers want to help save the planet. There's never been a better time to be cool and smart (as *in sync*) with selling pretty, upcycled things you make.

- Sales of sustainable products are growing twice those of other categories. (Nielsen)

- Over 90% percent of consumers around the world want to see brands support social and/or environmental issues. (WeAreFuterra.com)

- Over 60% of eco-conscious buyers believe earth-friendly items are better for their overall health. (Nielsen)

- More than 70% say they are buying more environmentally friendly products than they did five years ago. (Business News Daily)

- Lyst, a curator of fashion trends, reported a 75% increase in searches for sustainable-related keywords in 2019. (Lyst.com)

Supporting sustainable business is a mega-trend. The other big trend you will be tapping into is the demand for handmade products.

Etsy, the forerunner of selling handmade crafts online, just keeps growing year after year. Etsy expanded on average over 30% per year from 2013 to 2019. In stark contrast to many people losing their jobs and their homes in the terrible recession that began in October of 2008, Etsy sales rose and continued to rise during those tough economic times.

Eyeing Etsy's growth, in 2015 Amazon came up with their own Handmade marketplace.

The writing is on the wall. There's a real and growing demand for eco-friendly products you make yourself. The stories and statistics throughout these pages confirm it.

What's Covered in the Book

You will discover:

- Product ideas from upcycled or repurposed materials.

- What shoppers crave. Learn what's in demand before you start making.

- How to engage your family in a side gig everyone will love.

- How to price your products so you get top dollar and don't lose money.

- Where to find and stand out in multiple markets for your attractive, repurposed art and crafts.

- How to get free mentions in the media that send buyers to you.

- A marketing plan and calendar so you'll know what, how, and when to take actions.

- Online resources to tap into from wherever you live.

WHAT YOU NEED TO START

Unlike many small business ideas, starting an upcycled art or crafts gig is low-cost. Since most of your supplies are free, you only need time, simple tools, and a place to work.

If you don't have crafting skills, you can quickly learn them online for free. YouTube has videos on making upcycled DIY crafts with step-by-step instructions anyone can follow.

Need ideas for creating cool stuff to upcycle? Chapter 1 will get you started. Also, see hundreds of inspiring projects for recycled and upcycled art and crafts on the Pinterest board I put up to go with this book at: https://www.pinterest.com/JamesDillehay/repurposed-crafts/.

After you have filled your shelves and closets with things you have made, it's time to sell them at local art and craft shows. Craft shows get your upcycled products in front of loads of people and raking in fast sales.

You are about to discover a world of choices. But you don't have to do everything here and not all at the same time.

WHY THIS BOOK, WHY NOW

I love making cool stuff by hand. It's a great feeling when people buy my things and tell me what an artist I am. Ironic, since I didn't feel I had any creativity before I started on this path. Getting kudos for my work is almost as satisfying as getting paid. Almost.

I've displayed my handmade work at hugely popular craft shows, to stores and galleries from Manhattan to Sedona, on Etsy, Amazon, and eBay, and through my gallery. I was busy making and filling orders when the idea for this guide came unexpectedly.

A Facebook post caught my attention. It was a cartoon that read "Make America Greta Again." The joke came out of the media storm around Greta Thunberg's scathing speech to UN leaders. She tore into politicians about their being all talk and no action to help stop climate change. I wasn't in her audience, but her words set me on a new line of thinking.

Businesses, even small startups, are in a position to affect real change. One of my skillsets was helping others grow their handmade businesses. My crafts gallery in New

Mexico specialized in recycled art and craft items. Why don't I do something with what I have? I had skills, resources, and experiences that could help others.

For sure, making and selling art and craft from upcycled materials can make you money on the side. But there is an important side effect that helps the planet. Your small side business increases the power of the message: **reuse, reduce, recycle**.

You can make a difference!

The best place to begin is coming up with ideas for pretty upcycled things to make. Chapter 1 reveals a world of possibilities.

🔊 PURSES FROM USED CANDY WRAPPERS

```
I was excited to open my gallery in the tourist
destination of Madrid, New Mexico, but I didn't
have enough inventory. So, I bought from a
wholesaler of handmade items from Latin America.
Among the top sellers was a line of purses
made from upcycled candy wrappers. At first,
they didn't sell. Then I raised the prices and
shoppers started buying. It's true that shoppers
for handmade expect to pay more. If the price is
too low, they think the item is machine-made.
```

CHAPTER 1

Things to Make to Sell

There are thousands of possibilities for repurposed and sustainable things to make. This chapter shows you how to find ideas and how to prioritize them by products shoppers want.

Here you will learn about:
- How to find products in demand
- How to test-market your idea to shoppers
- How customers can give you new ideas
- Ways to make things that stand out from others
- Making reproducible vs one-of-a-kind items

The next section reveals how to research markets for product ideas already selling. **DO NOT COPY OTHERS' WORK**. It's not just unethical, you can lose your online web presence, or worse, be sued for copyright infringement. Use the sources here to brainstorm your own uniquely designed pieces.

HOW TO FIND PRODUCTS IN DEMAND

The top e-commerce sites for finding handmade products are Etsy and Amazon Handmade. We'll cover them in depth in later chapters. For now, you are about to discover how to mine these huge marketplaces for product ideas based what consumers are searching for and buying.

Search results below were from late 2019. Your results will differ. Keyword search data changes daily.

Etsy.com A search on Etsy for "recycled" products brought back over 300,000 listings. But that doesn't tell us which products shoppers are interested in. EtsyRank.com is a subscription service providing reports on keywords used by real buyers on Etsy and Google Shopping. Typing in the word "recycled" using EtsyRank's *Keyword Explorer* tool revealed:

Search Term	Etsy Searches	Clicks
recycled sweater mittens	19618	4154
recycled art	2321	11
recycled metal yard art	786	104
recycled jewelry	540	53
recycled tin earrings	533	42
recycled leather bag	516	303
recycled clothing	497	50
recycled skateboard	445	182
recycled earrings	404	110
soy candles recycled	335	43
recycled glass candle	322	171
recycled wool mittens	315	71
recycled wedding invitation	308	104
recycled metal art	287	82
recycled throw blanket	260	45

Explanation: the "Etsy Searches" column gives the number of searches in a thirty-day period for the "Search Term." The final column "Clicks" tell you how many searchers clicked through to a product listing.

The above is extracted from a report generated by EtsyRank for the search term "recycled." Note that "Clicks" are not sales, but a high number of click-throughs shows the strength of shopper interest. From the data above, several product ideas show potential.

📢 **CRAFT SUPPLIES ARE AMONG TOP SELLERS ON ETSY**

Art and craft supplies are one of the top sales categories on Etsy. A consumer demand worth exploring is creating earth-friendly craft supplies. Christopher Pourney, chosen as one of *Oprah's Favorite Things*, hand-produces a line of furniture restoration serums, waxes, and creams from organic and natural ingredients avoiding harmful artificial chemicals.

Amazon.com/handmade/ Amazon Handmade competes with Etsy. The test search results shown next came from the tool MerchantWords.com (subscription service).

Search Term	Amazon Searches in Handmade
recycled skateboard	5083
recycled bracelets for women	2310
recycled jewelry	1253
recycled glass earrings	898
recycled skateboard jewelry	756
recycled skateboard necklace	674
recycled glass necklace	650
recycled skateboard ring	643
recycled glass jewelry	538
recycled wine bottle platter	524
recycled vintage earrings	523
recycled bottle bracelet	500
recycled aluminum jewelry	468
gifts made from recycled materials	447
recycled earrings	391
recyclable jewelry	375
recycled jewelry for women	369
mens recycled ring	344

The above search results are for a thirty-day period in Amazon's Handmade category. Together with our earlier Etsy report, we now have a list of crafts to make that shoppers want.

Mining eBay Sales Data

eBay.com is probably not the site you first think of for selling handmade items. But before Etsy lured thousands of handmade sellers away with lower fees, it was the largest online market to list handcrafted pieces. The data below indicates eBay may still be an option for some makers.

The following are real searches looking for recycled and eco-friendly product opportunities on eBay. Not all product listings are true prospects, but many fit.

> Search term: "handmade"
> Filters: "sold items" plus "US only" (to eliminate cheap exports) Results: over 531,000 listings sold.
>
> Search term: "recycled"   Filters: same
> Results: 13,666 listings sold.
>
> Search term: "eco-friendly + handmade"   Filters: same
> Results: 2,387 listings sold.

Search term: "recycled art"   Filters: same
Results: 616 listings sold.

Search term: "upcycled"   Filters: same
Results: 382 listings sold.

DIY Upcycled + Recycled Craft Project Ideas

The websites below show upcycled craft ideas, some with how-to tutorials. The craft ideas you find here won't reveal sales potential or consumer demand data. That doesn't mean the items won't sell. See the checklist at the end of this chapter for making products stand out.

For hundreds of ideas for recycled and upcycled art and crafts see my Pinterest board at: https://www.pinterest.com/JamesDillehay/repurposed-crafts/.

Recyclart.org Thousands of project ideas (some with detailed plans) for recycling everyday objects into arts and crafts products.

HGTV.com/design/topics/upcycling Lots of projects to upcycle, reuse, repurpose items for the home and for wearing.

YouTube.com Search YouTube for "recycled crafts" or "upcycled crafts" to find plenty of projects, many of them DIY tutorial videos.

Upcycled Craft Ideas by Category

Another brainstorming technique for things to make from recycled materials is to search in categories on Etsy. Go to Etsy.com. Under the search bar, you will see major categories. Clicking on each will get you a drop-down menu with sub-categories.

Make a list of categories under which you could make products with upcycled or sustainable materials. Prioritize items. Pick things you will enjoy making. You can be profitable with just one or two types of products. Add new items as your business grows.

Original Ideas Sell

Don't overlook your original creativity when it comes to thinking about what to make. My best-selling product line was based on an accessory scarf I saw lots of women wearing. But all the versions I came across looked plain and boring. I created an artistic adaptation with lots of color and texture. My craft show and Etsy customers loved them, especially the scarves made from upcycled fibers. My scarves sold well because they were beautiful, not because consumers were already searching for them.

📢 **SURFERS TAKE ON OCEAN PLASTIC**

Two guys on a surfing trip to Bali discovered a beach awash with plastic garbage. And more was flowing in hourly. They decided something needed to be done, so they created 4ocean, a company with a mission to reduce plastic waste in our oceans. They create and sell bracelets made from recycled plastic and glass bottles. They donate at least 1% of their revenues to nonprofit environmental conservation groups. They've been written about in Forbes and Newsweek. Read more about them at 4ocean.com

---

How to Test Market Your Product Idea

Art and Craft Shows

The fastest real-life testing ground for handmade products is to display them at two or three well-attended art and craft shows. Art and craft shows allow you to get immediate feedback through shopper comments and sales.

Social Media

Another place to test your idea is on sites like Instagram, Pinterest, and Facebook. Post images or videos of your products. Be sure to include tags like #upcycled, #sustainable, #recycled, etc. Find more hashtags related to your items with Hashtagify.me. Your social media contacts know you—or kind of know you—so they may be more supportive than unbiased. Even so, many Etsy stores have grown their customer base starting with sales from friends, family, and social media connections.

How Customers Give You Product Ideas

Shoppers can be a fountain of new product ideas. Pay attention to their comments. The scarf line that I described above I made in 25 color combinations, but shoppers would sometimes ask for other colors. Every time I filled one of these special requests, I'd make extras because it was a more efficient use of my time and I wanted to see how the public responded to the new colors. Several times the specially-requested color combo outsold the others.

Early on, several customers said they were buying a scarf as a gift and wanted to tell the recipient how to wear it. So, I started including a "how to wear" instruction card to go with each scarf.

Since more and more customers were buying gifts, I began packaging and displaying the scarves in a gift box with the "how to wear" card.

Important takeaway: I was no longer only *in the scarf market*, I was also *in the gift market*.

If I hadn't listened to my customers, I would have overlooked the above ideas that boosted my sales more than any marketing tactic.

Making Reproducible Versus One-of-a-Kind Products

When thinking about items to make and sell, there are two options:

Create products that can be produced again and again. You might change colors or materials to improve them but the product line remains basically duplicatable. An example would be handbags made from recycling inner tubes. There might be some material difference between pieces, but you follow a pattern and create the same basic item again and again.

Or, *make one-of-a-kind products*. Examples include art pieces like sculptures, wall hangings, unique furniture, etc.

THINGS TO MAKE TO SELL

> 📣 **HELP FOLKS CREATE PROJECTS TO MEMORIALIZE A LOVED ONE**
>
> "I wish my dad could have seen the 3-D photographic memory box I made after he died, for he would have been proud of me for practicing what he always preached; namely that everything has value, even something that looks like junk. To others who searched through daddy's garage after his death for tools they wanted to keep, the stack of grease-covered tractor gaskets back in the corner was just filthy junk. But I saw artistry in the shape of those gaskets, and when I scratched the surface of one and found it to be copper, I could almost hear daddy saying, "See that copper? It has value. Save it." I saw all the small and large holes in it as a perfect picture frame. It took me a week to clean the grime from the gasket and restore its copper tones, and I think even daddy would have been surprised to see how beautiful it turned out to be. Like him, in fact. On the surface, daddy looked scruffy, but when you scratched a bit, you found a beautiful person with a heart as big as the world." - Barbara Brabec, author *Marcella's Secret Dreams and Stories: A Mother's Legacy*. Visit BarbaraBrabec.com

It's not an either/or choice. You can do both, but be aware of how the decision will affect your business.

- Listing one-of-a-kind items for sale online requires taking photos for every new unique piece you make. If you sell at art fairs, photos aren't as critical to the sale since shoppers see your pieces up close.

- A reproducible products business can be scaled. You can sell again and again because you have a consistent product line. Making one-of-a-kind products usually means marketing to galleries and building your brand as an artist. Reproducible product lines have predictable production costs, whereas making one-of-a-kind products requires figuring costs and prices for each new piece. See Chapter 5 on pricing.

- You can create and improve a system for reproducing products over and over. But one-of-a-kind products may require an unpredictable and therefore more lengthy production process.

Many makers grow careers as artists this route because it feeds a creative need. In my early years, I had both a production line and then sometimes branched off into making one-of-a-kind, large pieces to expand my design skills.

Finding Raw Materials

The first place to look for materials is in your recycling bin or your garage. Examples include: junk mail, newspapers, magazines, CDs and cases, cardboard boxes, plastic bags, bottle caps, drinking straws, glass and plastic bottles, clothes and accessories, dryer sheets, egg cartons, and mosaic tiles.

As your business grows and you run out of your own home's supply of materials, ask your neighbors.

Go around to local businesses to learn what they throw away that you could use for raw materials.

Some makers use materials found in nature, like interesting-looking tree branches, seashells, sand dollars, flowers, herbs, stones and crystals.

Other sources of cheap supplies include: garage sales, junkyards, construction sites and homes undergoing remodeling. Wear gloves and safety glasses when rummaging through piles of trash.

The US Environmental Protection Agency posts a list of reources for students and teachers looking to reduce, reuse, and recycle at: https://www.epa.gov/recycle/reduce-reuse-recycle-resources-students-and-educators

Checklist for Making Products Stand Out

After you have your product list, the next step is making things. How will you craft them so they stand out from other sellers? The following list will help:

- [ ] *Your story.* People love products that help a cause, so explain how your work helps the environment. Your story is the connector to shoppers' desires to support earth-friendly businesses.

- [ ] *Quality sells.* Whatever you make, do it well. Quality work is obvious and attractive.

- [ ] *Colors.* Next to quality, color plays a major role in standing out over similar but competing products. If you are good (as in: your work is selling) at putting colors together, you have a huge advantage. For those without training in working with color, see the book, *Color Works* by Deb Minz.

- [ ] *Themes.* Design your product line around a niche or theme. Many of your customers will have someone on their gift list who collects dinosaurs, unicorns, elephants, gnomes, or other collectibles.

- [ ] *Personalization.* Personalized gifts are very popular, both at craft shows and on Etsy. If appropriate for what you make, offer the option to add a recipient's name to an item for a premium price. Some top-selling products on Etsy and Amazon Handmade offer customizing or personalizing as an option.

- [ ] *Inform shoppers you use upcycled or sustainable materials.* Don't assume customers will know that you use recycled or sustainable materials. Point it out in promotional material like hangtags, packaging, websites, and art fair booth displays.

- [ ] *Packaging.* Packaging is a place to brand your business. It's also a way to use sustainable materials (call attention to this on your boxes and wrappers) as many companies that make packaging boxes and bags do so with recycled paper.

- [ ] *Eye-catching images.* When listing your products online, your images do the selling (*or not.*) If there is any place in your business that justifies investing money, it is in getting great photos of your work. See Appendix 1 for resources.

SELL ARTS & CRAFTS FROM UPCYCLED MATERIALS

> 📣 **SCRAP CREATIVE REUSE: CREATIVE EXPRESSION WITH RECLAIMED MATERIALS**
>
> With rising consumer concern about the environmental impact of their purchases, creative makers see reuse centers as a resource for finding raw resuable materials. SCRAP Creative Reuse is a nonprofit network of creative reuse centers. The team at SCRAP helps foster and offer support to new reuse centers with best practices to get them up and running. Six cities in the US have SCRAP network stores Portland, OR, Baltimore, MD, Ann Arbor, MI, Denton, TX, Arcata, CA, and Richmond, VA. Their mission: creative expression with reclaimed materials. See scrapcreativereuse.org

Now that you have ways to find product ideas, you are close to starting your side hustle. What will it look like? Read on for a glimpse into how a new creative upcycling venture could evolve.

> **MORE UPCYCLE PRODUCT IDEAS:**
>
> - Paint used bicycle wheels in multi colors and attach each to a pole and then place in garden areas.
> - Make candle lanterns from old tin cans by punching holes in unique patterns.
> - Take old calendar images and glue to square tiles to quickly become attractive table coasters.
> - Turn an unused baby crib into a magazine rack.
> - Repurpose old sweaters into pillow covers.

CHAPTER 2

What a Side Hustle Might Look Like

Before we get into the step-by-steps of growing your side hustle, this chapter tells a fictional account based on how a venture might look in a family situation.

Having family support for your recycling gig can be a great plus. It feels safer knowing someone's got your back. Even if you are a solo entrepreneur, you will probably interact with family members along the way. Getting them involved can take your venture to a whole new level.

There are pros and cons for doing any kind of gig with your family. However, we can take a clue for why a upcycled products business stands a good chance of working from what's happening in school systems.

If you Google "recycled art," many of the results are links to news stories covering local school contests. Teachers and parents see these contests as a way to motivate kids to get creative and to appreciate the environment.

Other compelling reasons you may want your family in on your gig:

- ✓ What family can't use extra money every month?
- ✓ Sharing an opportunity with your family creates a bond through doing creative projects together that help the planet.
- ✓ If you are a resident and have a business in the US, adults can legally hire their children and pay them up to $12,200 tax-free (source: Nolo.com.)
- ✓ Creativity is good for everyone. Selling things you make raises self-esteem.

SELL ARTS & CRAFTS FROM UPCYCLED MATERIALS

- ✓ Young people can help earn their own money for college.
- ✓ Young people are probably more motivated to reuse and recycle and to have a sense of urgency to help the environment.

Note: Kids under 18 need parental management to open an Etsy or other online store.

📢 **SCULPTING PLASTIC, RAISING AWARENESS**

```
Swapna Namboodiri, a software engineer by
education and now artist by profession, grew
up in India and lives in Qatar. Swapna is a
plastic sculptor whose mission is to create
artworks from discarded plastics and raise
awareness of the impact plastics have on the
planet. Not a formally trained artist, she grew
in confidence as her work found its way into
private collections. Her sculptural artworks
are themed around "ocean life" since the seas
are affected so adversely by plastic pollution.
Source: ILoveQatar.net
```

THE FAMILY SIDE HUSTLE

Marianne Welder is fourteen years old. She entered her middle school recycled-art contest and won first prize. Her local TV station ran a story on the contest and the winners, featuring Marianne and her art piece. Her parents proudly tell everyone in the family, who all get excited.

The town newspaper also did a story on the event, which included a photo shoot and brief piece on Marianne and why she entered the contest. Marianne answers, "We can all do more to save the planet. I wanted to show my own way to help."

The word is getting around about Marianne's big win. Friends of the family call and ask if Marianne makes smaller items as gifts. They would like to buy some.

She plays with ideas and comes up with a line of small animal figurines made by upcycling junk. Unicorns are her favorite so she puts extra effort into them.

Marianne's twelve-year old brother, Jason, doesn't want to be left out. He's also got some cool ideas for recycling stuff to sell.

Marianne asks her mom and dad, Ann and John, if they will sign off on an Etsy store if Marianne runs it as a small business. Everyone agrees it's a great idea. The new venture is off and running.

Meanwhile, Ann's friends congratulate her on her daughter's efforts. Ann used to host Tupperware parties, so she has the idea that a home party might be a way for Marianne to show off her new upcycled craft gifts and earn a little extra money.

Marianne didn't have to pay for her materials, since her things are made throw-aways. But she still has to come up with a price. She goes online and browses Etsy and Amazon Handmade to learn what others charge for similar items. That, at least, gives her a starting price.

As her business grows, Marianne uses a pricing formula to make sure she accounts for all her time when making her pieces.

Back at the home party, ten neighbors and friends show up. Refreshments are available and Marianne's and some of Jason's crafts are displayed around the table.

Marianne talks about how she makes her upcycled animals. She sells three (two of them are unicorns) and also gets lots of praise for her creativity. Everyone is getting excited about her side hustle.

Like many girls her age, Marianne spends a few hours a day on social media. She uploads pictures of her upcycled gifts to Instagram and Twitter. The images get liked and retweeted by her friends, and then by some of their friends.

Marianne's grandfather comes across the book you are reading now and thinks it would be the perfect gift to help her in her little business. Clever guy. Marianne reads in it how to link her Instagram and other posts to her Etsy store. Two of her first round of social shares turn into sales.

She also learns about a cool app called EtsyRank. After convincing her parents the $10-per-month subscription would pay for itself, she uses it to discover words and phrases Etsy buyers use when shopping. Now she has more and better tags to include on her Etsy product listings.

Marianne is getting more and more excited but she feels uncertain about what to do next. She asks her dad who thinks maybe it's time for a family sit down to discuss options.

John does some research and learns that in the US, a child can earn up to $12,200 a year (in 2019) without having to pay income tax.

This gives Ann and John an idea. What if they start a real business that Marianne could eventually take over when she reaches eighteen. Expenses (like a home-office deduction) could be legally deducted from income and the family might get some tax breaks.

📢 **FROM AC REPAIR TO RECYCLING ARTIST**

```
AlJohn Farquharson learned welding working
in his father's air conditioning business.
He repurposes copper sheets, pipes and other
materials he finds at scrap yards and welds them
into artworks. He got started when he needed a
last-minute present for his wife. Too late to
buy a gift, he created a copper flower planter.
AlJohn has since crafted a wide range of copper
art structures, including a standing alligator
and a man fishing in a boat. Also a musician, he
has made a copper violin and a copper guitar
he plays. Source: CommunityNewspapers.com. For
information about AlJohn Farquharson, visit
Facebook.com/raokmiami/
```

John's accountant friend confirms it is possible and tells him to keep records, come up with a name for their business, open a separate business checking account, and get a business license and sales tax permit. He also cautions John to get a zoning permit waiver if they plan to run the business from home.

After talking it over, the family agrees to call the business Welder Creative, as no one else has registered the name. Naming it after the family allows anyone who wants to contribute to take part.

Because Marianne and Jason are minors, John and Ann must set up the legal stuff, like opening a bank account for the business and setting up a phone app to accept credit cards.

Ann gets the permits because John has a full-time job and she only works part-time while both kids are in school. Now it's official: Welder Creative is a legitimate business. The family feels excited and a little nervous.

Marianne and now Jason are making things almost every day. Sales on Etsy are coming in but slowly. Marianne looks around her room one day and realizes she has way too many things made. Where can she sell more pieces?

Since everyone's off for the weekends, they reserve a booth space at a local crafts show coming up. They get a pop-up tent and set it up in the garage so they can play with design ideas for the booth. After a few disagreements about how to display their stuff, they go on Pinterest and find examples of cool displays they all like.

As the show weekend nears, everyone is looking forward to the event. Ann has set up a SquareUp account in the business name so they can use a credit card reader with their mobile phone to accept payments.

Marianne and Jason have taken lots of photos, and made signs and posters to put around the booth. Marianne also posts her first-place award from the school contest.

When the craft show starts on a Saturday morning, the whole family is there. They quickly see the booth is not large enough for both the family and the shoppers so they agree to take shifts. Those not working the booth can wander around the show.

Shoppers show up around 10 a.m. Marianne is a little disappointed to find some people walking right by their booth without giving their display a glance. She's beginning to wonder if she hasn't made a big mistake.

Then around 11:30, a woman walks into the booth and starts talking. "How beautiful! What an artist you are!" Marianne says "thank you" and is about to tell her story when the woman says "I have to go but I'll be back" and then rushes away.

Marianne is almost in tears. All the work she put into her pieces and building the display—no one wants her work. Why did she bother?

Ann sees her daughter's dismay and is reminded of how she felt when she began trying to sell Tupperware. Ann tells Marianne, "Honey, we have to be patient. Your pieces aren't for everyone. We're here waiting for the right customers who see how special your work is."

The next couple that came into the booth bought a piece and said they wanted a business card so they could go home and think about gifts to order later online.

More people come and go and Marianne's mood rises as sales and praise trickle in. Jason can hardly contain himself when two of his pieces sell.

Around 2 p.m., the crowd thins. But vendors have to stay open until 5 p.m. according to the show rules. Around 4 p.m., the woman who first came into the booth early in the day returns and says "I'm so glad you are still here. I want this one and this one." She pointed to her choices.

At the end of the show, everyone is a little tired but also happy, because they sold three times the cost of the booth.

📢 WELDER TURNS JUNK INTO ART

Aidan Keefe Rayner welds discarded metal pieces into beautiful sculptures. His work spans a variety of themes, including florals and animals. Working as a heavy machine operator at a junkyard gave him a daily view of rubbish he transforms into artistic, keepsake treasures. His first art opening show at a local gallery on Whidbey Island almost sold out. See his work at facebook.com/aidan.k.rayner. Source: SouthWhidbeyRecord.com

---

John asks, "You guys up for another event? I just heard from one of the other sellers about a big show next month in a nearby city. We could make an adventure out of it."

Jason was all in, but Marianne was a little reluctant. She said she needed to think about it some more.

On Monday, her Etsy store gets two orders and a nice message from the couple that took her business card at the event. Marianne suddenly saw the potential from doing more shows.

Over the coming months, the family grew together around the venture. Naturally, the family disagreed about some decisions, but usually came together on most points.

Sales grew as did their mailing list, because they collected e-mail addresses from customers and admirers. At the end of the first year of their side hustle, they had 134 customer names. Whenever they came out with a new product or would have a booth in a local event, they sent out announcements.

Ahead of tax time the following year, John presented the bookkeeping records to his accountant. It turned out their side business had made a profit. A large amount of the profit was offset by expenses, like travel and booth fees. It was kind of like getting paid to take the family to new places on working vacations.

After the first year of their side hustle, everyone agreed it was worth going on. The second year, a new market opportunity opened up.

At the better-attended art and craft shows, a shop or gallery owner who had been browsing the event for new artists would see Welder Creative's display and ask if they wholesaled. Though at first they didn't know how to respond, one kind store owner explained how wholesale worked and offered to take some pieces on consignment to see how her customers reacted. The revenue split was 50/50 and the Welders would get paid the month following the sale.

The shop owner explained that the Welder pieces could get much higher prices in galleries, but if they did shows in the same city, their show prices would have to match the gallery prices. The family soon found themselves growing a wholesale business and building a name for themselves as artists.

From his earnings, Jason bought himself a new smartphone. He used it to take even better pictures and videos of his cool upcycled crafts, which got lots of likes and even some sales.

> 📢 **RECYCLING COUPLE OPENS GALLERY**
>
> Husband-and-wife team, Elizabeth and Sam Steffey opened a gallery for their recycled art in Valdese, NC, partly because they were getting too many visitors arriving at their home to see their work. Sam is a metal worker who fashions artistic pieces from old metal and other objects. They have received commissions from organizations like the American Heart Association. Their gallery, Sam's Recycled Art, also showcases other local artists who work with sustainable and repurposed materials. One artisan refurbishes furniture that would have gone to junkyards. A glass worker rescues old glass and refashions it into new art pieces. Source: Morganton.com/news/ See Sam's Recycled gallery at: Facebook.com/SamsRecycled/

Marianne put some of her earnings away for college. Some went to continue growing her "side hustle turned professional business." She was proud of what she helped build and happy her family was part of it. She made her story part of her marketing material in the hope that others would be inspired to create a business that made a difference.

Your side hustle will grow in ways you cannot predict. But, the next chapter helps you get started the right way so you can forestall problems with the IRS and local governments.

> **MORE UPCYCLE PRODUCT IDEAS:**
>
> - Paint old picture frames in different colors and use as wall art or shelf decor.
> - Arrange used crayons to form single letter shapes (as in someone's initials), glue to corrugated back, and frame for personalized wall art.
> - Weave old leather belts as a seat for used chair.

CHAPTER 3

Setting Up to Do Business

To get your gig started in the right direction, take steps to protect your business name, stay in line with government regulations, and set up how you will accept payments.

This chapter explains the basic legal requirements for US residents. For readers in other countries, check your local business requirements.

For most young adults under 18 years old, a parent or guardian will have to sign for you when setting up checking accounts or applying for permits.

Here you will learn about:
- Choosing a name for your business
- Legal requirements: permits and licenses
- Accepting credit card payments
- Keeping records

CHOOSING A NAME FOR YOUR BUSINESS

Your side hustle business needs a name that is short, catchy, memorable, and doesn't already belong to someone else.

Many makers use their own name as their business name. There are good reasons for this. For one, it's more personal; customers feel you are a real person standing behind your name.

Another plus for using your name is that it makes it easy for customers who have bought from you at craft shows to recognize your name when it appears on their receipt and credit card statement. It happens that someone making a lot of credit card purchases at an event doesn't remember all the business names and then disputes the charge later after going over their monthly statement.

If you don't want to use your name, be selective about an alternative. Make a list of your favorites with the best one at the top. Then wait a few days for your ideas to settle before coming back to it. If you still like your choice after time has passed, the next step is to learn if the name is already in use.

Go online and check to see if anyone else is already using it. A Google search is usually a good place to start.

If Google doesn't return a link with your ideal business name, next check for registered trademarks at www.uspto.gov/trademarks/process/search/.

If you don't find your prospective name registered as a trademark, then do a business name search in your state. Do this by searching the phrase "business name availability (your state's name)." Usually, this search will bring up your state's business filings bureau where you can learn if anyone else is already using the name you have in mind.

📣 **A CATCHY BUSINESS NAME**

The Lip Bar, a cleverly named handmade business, started when founder Melissa Butler got fed up with all the chemicals in commercial beauty products. Her handmade, all-natural lipstick line found its way onto *Shark Tank* and *The Bethenny Show*.

After you have done the research and confirm that no one else is already using your ideal business name, register it with a business license.

Legal Requirements: Permits and Licenses

Setting up a business differs from country to country. If you live outside the US, see the end of this section.

For most businesses that don't sell food or alcohol, there are usually four registrations or permits you need to operate legally in the US.

Zoning permit waiver. Most side hustles will be run from home, which is more than likely in a residential area. Your home probably isn't zoned for doing business. However, you may still be allowed to operate with a zoning waiver as long as your home business activity doesn't draw attention or get complaints from neighbors. Visit your city or county zoning office to learn what's required.

Local business license. Apply at your local county business registration office. Locate yours at: https://www.sba.gov/business-guide/launch-your-business/apply-licenses-permits

State sales tax permit. In the US, except for Alaska, Delaware, Montana, New Hampshire and Oregon, all other states require a state sales tax permit for selling products or services in the respective area. To learn where to get a sales tax permit in your state, do an online search for "(your state name) sales tax permit." Usually the state sales tax permit is free. Once you are signed up, the state sends you forms to fill out and return with any sales tax collected. If you will sell at festivals and art and craft shows, most events require a state sales tax permit.

Federal Employer Identification number (EIN.) If your business doesn't have employees, you may not need an EIN. Sole proprietors can use their social security number when reporting business income to the IRS. If you hire others, you'll need the EIN. Apply online at https://ein-forms-gov.com/

Starting a Business Outside the US

For starting and registering a business in Canada, see-canada.ca/en/services/business/start.html

For the UK, visit www.gov.uk.

For Australia, start at register.business.gov.au. Then see business.gov.au/info/run/tax/what-taxes-do-i-need-to-register-for

Within the European Union: see europa.eu/youreurope/business/running-business/start-ups/starting-business/index_en.htm

For other countries, Google the phrase "how to legally start a business in (insert your country name)."

Accepting Credit Card Payments

If you sell at home parties, farmer's markets or craft fairs, a mobile creditccard reader allows you to accept credit card payments through your mobile phone or notebook.

If you plan to sell on Etsy or Amazon Handmade, you won't need your own credit card processor as they handle transactions and pass on the processing fee to you.

Does accepting credit cards make a difference? For art and craft shows, the answer is a definite yes. My sales more than doubled when I began accepting cards. I'm not alone. A survey showed 83% of businesses report it increased sales.

Almost 80% of shoppers prefer using a credit card. Fortunately, technology has made it easy to accept credit cards from just about anywhere. Using a small card reader that plugs into your smart phone and an app from your card processor, you will key in an item, swipe or insert the card, and have the buyer sign with their finger or a stylus pen.

Two popular mobile credit card service providers among craft show vendors are Square at https://squareup.com and PayPal at https://www.paypal.com/us/business/pos-system/card-reader. Both services allow you to accept credit card payments through your smart phone, with no monthly charges and only a per-transaction fee. Money from a sale minus the fee is deposited directly into your checking account.

Keeping Records / Accounting

This guide will show you many markets to sell your work in. You will want to keep records of your sales by market, along with your expenses, to track which venues are the most profitable.

Another important reason to account for sales and expenses is that even as a small, part-time business, the IRS requires you to keep records and file income tax, even when you don't show a profit.

There are different ways of keeping records. If you have a smartphone, there are apps like *Expensify* that allow you to snap photos of your receipts. If you prefer to make entries by hand, log books for tracking expenses can be found at office supply stores and bookstores. TaxJar.com integrates with Etsy shops making it easy to record sales data. Other accounting tools include: Wave, QuickBooks Self-Employed, GoDaddy Bookkeeping for Etsy Sellers, and Zoho.

Examples of expenses you may be allowed to deduct from your business income include: business-related insurance, show rental fees, bank charges, trade periodicals, advertising, office supplies, utilities, contract labor, salaries, equipment rentals or repairs, depreciation, and the cost of goods sold.

For more tax advantages from your craft business, see *How to Price Crafts and Things You Make to Sell*.

> 📢 **LOCAL DEMAND FOR ECO-FRIENDLY GROWS**
>
> Old City Knoxville is home to The Old City Market. Many of the artisans exhibiting their art and crafts make their work using low-waste and ethical sources. Though the market isn't promoted as an "eco-friendly" fair, a lot of the vendors use recycled materials, which is a big draw. Source: UTDailyBeacon.com

Once you have an accounting system in place, it's a good practice to back up your files regularly and store them safely. After a computer failed and wiped all my data, I now keep two sets of external hard-drive backups and one online backup account.

Create a Production Logbook

Keeping a production logbook helps when it comes time to reproduce an item. In my logbook, I include a picture or drawing of each piece with details of material costs, production time, finished dimensions, how well an item sold and other notes.

Legal and accounting stuff may seem tedious, but doing it right means you can relax and move forward without the worry of getting in trouble with the government. Now let's look at how to prepare your handmade products to make the best presentation to shoppers.

CHAPTER 4

Preparing to Market Your Hustle

If you were going on a first date and wanted to impress the other person, you would likely take extra steps with grooming and dressing. Likewise, when getting your products ready to market, there are "grooming and dressing" tips for making them stand out and increase engagement.

This chapter teaches you how to impress shoppers with photos, promotional material, and packaging. While your upcycled products can sell themselves when displayed at art or craft shows, in other markets like selling online or to galleries and stores, images and presentations have to sell for you.

Promotional material gives you a way to pass along branding cues so customers remember and refer others to you. Branding cues include style elements like fonts, colors, and icons that go into your signage, business cards, hangtags, web pages, and more. Once your branding cues are created, you can repurpose them again and again.

BRANDING CUES

First impressions are often lasting ones, including brand names and logos. The following elements make shoppers feel more confident about doing business with you.

- ☐ *Your Authenticity.* Big companies have a problem conveying authenticity. Corporations don't have souls. As a small business, you can be authentic, that's your brand. No one else is like you. Your choices around logos, fonts, colors, and images can reflect your personality.

- [ ] *Your Business Name.* We discussed the importance of naming your business in Chapter 2. After you've settled on the name you intend to use, it should appear throughout your promotional material.

- [ ] *Images.* Images tell stories. They deliver visuals when you are marketing online and for your display when you are at arts or crafts shows. You need: product-only images with a white background for online store listings, how-it's-made images, how-it's-used images if needed, lifestyle images showing people enjoying your item, jury images when applying to arts, and crafts fairs and pictures of you to accompany your artist's story. See Appendix 1 for more on photos.

- [ ] *Your Artist Story.* Even if you've just started making and selling things, you can refer to yourself as an artist or artisan. Maybe you knew from an early age you wanted to make quilts and now you create beautiful art quilts from discarded T-shirts to inspire others to be more sustainable. People relate to stories. Mass-manufactured things rarely connect us to real people behind the products. The *buy-handmade* and *save-the-planet* trends reveal that shoppers are rejecting factory-made products in favor of individual creativity.

- [ ] *Your Logo and Icon.* A logo is a small visual that expresses a feeling you want to convey to shoppers. Some sellers make a smaller version of their logo to use as a website icon. Free online tools like <u>Canva.com</u> and <u>Snappa.com</u> help you design your own.

- [ ] *Your Elevator Pitch.* In a few short sentences (30 seconds or less to say) what does your upcycled product promise customers? For example, an upcycled handbag maker promises buyers a "*fashion accessory from material destined for landfills.*" The maker isn't just selling handbags, she's promising shoppers a way to help the environment; something more and more shoppers care about.

☐ *Fonts and Colors.* Consistency is part of good branding. Choose fonts and colors that remain consistent through all your printed materials and website content.

☐ *Your Contact Information.* Every message you send or promote through should contain information on how people can easily reach you, including your website, phone number, e-mail, and address.

📣 RECYCLING ARTIST TELLS STORIES

Since 1996, Mitch Berg has worked with fused and lampwork glass, adding elements of welded scrap metal, altered wood, and found objects to create one-of-a-kind constructions. His work tells stories of humor and humanity, delighting audiences and building a solid collector base. Since 2001, Mitch has participated in art shows across the country at which his colorful creations have received many awards. Read more about him at MitchBergArt.com. Mitch founded and runs FUEGO, a multi-media art studio school in Albuquerque. Artists can collaborate, have access to tools, and improve their skills through workshops. Like Mitch's artwork made from found objects, Fuego Studio is built from converted shipping containers, a disused semi-truck, and an abandoned building. See FuegoABQ.com

---

TYPES OF PROMOTIONAL MATERIALS

Integrate the elements above into your promotional messaging using:

☐ **Videos.** Tell your artist story with video. Video rules over online marketing. Over 70% (and rising) of shoppers say video influenced their purchases. Over 90% of watchers are likely to remember a call-to-action on a video. Etsy, Amazon, and most social sites support and encourage product videos to increase sales. Repurpose your video content into podcasts, blog posts, tweets, and social posts.

☐ **Business cards** are among the entrepreneur's cheapest yet most useful tools. Imagine you are wearing something you made from upcycled material and someone says, *"that is so cute, where did you get it?"* You are ready with a business card with all your contact information.

☐ **Hangtags**. Every piece you sell should have a hanging tag that gives details about your product: the way you made it, simple instructions for product care when appropriate, and something like the words "handmade by" your name.

☐ **Thank-You cards**. With every sale, including a signed *Thank-You* card is a warm, personal touch that customers will appreciate because so many sellers neglect to do it. Include your logo and contact info on the back. When I pack an online order to send out, I place a *Thank-You* card with a coupon for a discount off the customer's next order.

☐ **Packaging**. Packaging is another opportunity to message your commitment to the environment. Use (and tell customers that you use): biodegradable packaging peanuts, upcycled corrugated cardboard, recycled paper, or other biodegradable organic materials.

☐ **Signs and banners**. If you do art or craft shows, expos, or even home parties, use signs and banners. Many office supply stores can take your PDF file and create a sign with foam board backing, lamination and grommet holes for hanging for a reasonable price. Include your business name, a brief blurb or positive review quote, and your website address on your signs.

☐ **Postcards** printed on recycled paper are low-cost reminders to mail to previous customers. Cards can include an eye-catching image on one side and marketing message, name, address, and website on the other side. Postcards can help sell new products and close-outs. Mail cards periodically to your customer list. Send out invitational notecards to your mailing list whenever you will be back in their area to do a show or home party.

- [ ] **Certificates of authenticity.** If you make limited editions, one-of-a-kind items, or other series work that builds your brand as an artist, include *Certificates of Authenticity*. Print them on quality recycled paper.

- [ ] **Your voice mail message.** If you don't always answer your phone, your voice mail message can communicate a marketing message. Include your website address and perhaps information about an upcoming craft show where you will be displaying.

- [ ] **Checks, return address labels, sales receipts, gift certificates, order forms, sticker labels** provide more opportunities to add a logo, website and promo blurb about what you do. When at art and craft shows, my customer receives an e-mail or text receipt that includes my business name, photo of me, and contact information so they can easily remember who they made the purchase from.

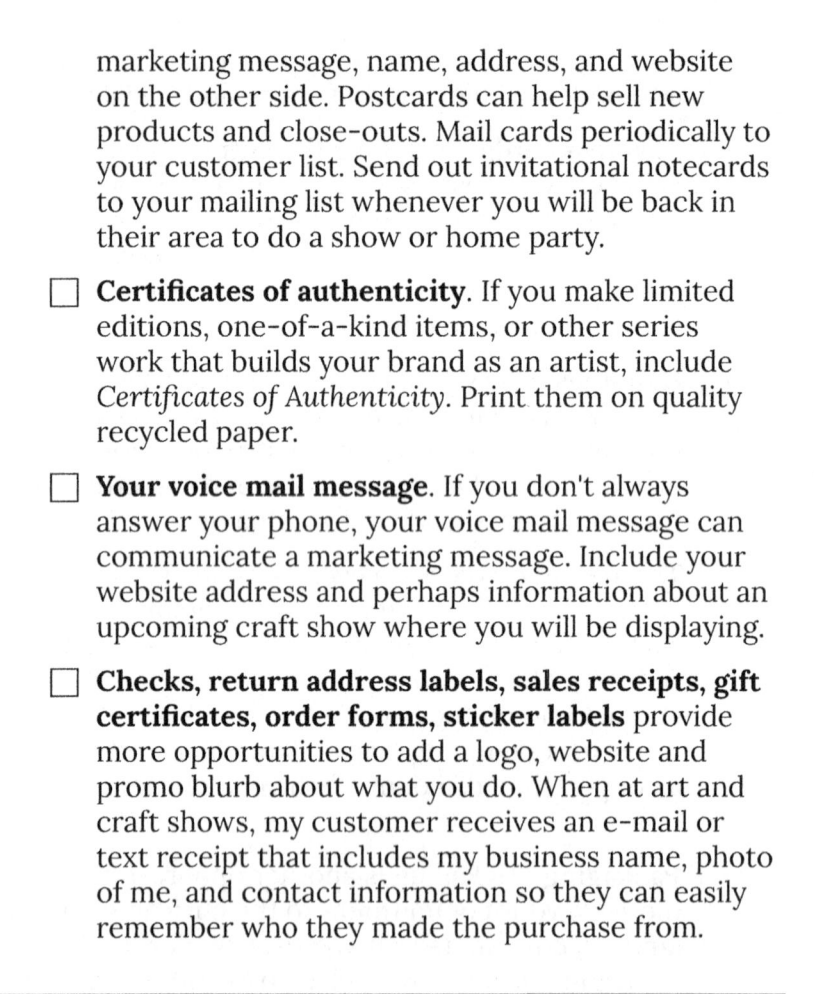

📢 **MAKE AND SELL ECO-WRAPPING**

```
You don't have to make a recycled craft to make
money. There's a huge demand for earth-friendly
packaging. Some Etsy sellers offer wrapping made
from recycled silk saris and other materials.
```

DESIGN RESOURCES

Good design in your marketing materials is as important as good product images. If you want to design your own, the sites here help with easy-to-use templates:

DesignBold.com
Canva.com
GetStencil.com
Snappa.com
Fotor.com

I've found examples of creative packaging at:

Flickr.com/search/?q=packaging
Pinterest.com (search for "packaging design creative.")

It's worth investing in professional-looking materials. Find graphic designers to do design for you at:

CreativeMarket.com
MockupEditor.com
DesignHill.com
CrowdSpring.com
Fiverr.com
99Designs.com
HatchWise.com (logos)
Etsy.com Search for "logo design" or "banner design" or "etsy shop makeover"

Printing Services

VistaPrint.com
GotPrint.com
Moo.com
Printique.com

Preparing your side hustle for prime time has probably given you ideas for what to do next. Before you go further, though, we need to price your handmade pieces so you make a good profit. Keep reading to get the insider's look into the best pricing formula and strategy.

```
       MORE UPCYCLE PRODUCT IDEAS:

 •  Collect mason jars, add soil and plant herbs
    for mini herb gardens.
```

CHAPTER 5

How to Price Upcycled Art & Crafts

This chapter teaches you how to price your products. Coming up with a fair price requires a little math, but making the effort will pay you back many times over. Knowing your profit margins guides your choices in where and what you will sell, and how you grow your side hustle.

What you will learn:
- Understanding retail and wholesale pricing
- Discovering how much will shoppers pay
- How much does it cost to make an item
- The pricing formula
- Your profit margin
- Pricing one-of-a-kind items
- Installation charges
- Lowering your production costs

UNDERSTANDING RETAIL AND WHOLESALE PRICING

You may sell your handmade pieces in several markets like on Etsy or Amazon, in gift shops, at home parties, at art and craft shows, to interior designers, through galleries, or mail-order catalogs. These markets fall into one of two categories: retail or wholesale. This section describes the different approaches for pricing in each category.

Retail pricing is the amount you ask for a piece when you are selling direct to a customer. Examples of places you might sell retail include art and craft shows, festivals, online through a website, home parties, or from your own studio.

Wholesale pricing is the amount you charge for items you sell to someone else who resells your products to their customers. For instance, stores, galleries, and mail-order catalogs like Sundance Catalog are wholesale markets. Stores price items two to two-and-a-half times what they pay for them.

If you plan to grow your business by selling to stores, knowing your costs and your prices tells you if you can afford to sell wholesale. Imagine having fifty or more stores around the country showing your items five to seven days a week.

There's no definitive answer to whether wholesale or retail is a better business model. I know makers who will not do craft shows, choosing instead to work from home. I know others who only do shows or sell online and never wholesale. And there are other sellers like me who do both.

📢 **QUILTS FROM T-SHIRTS**

Finding a niche can set your recycled products business apart. Cozy Quilts and MemoryStitch offer custom quilts assembled and sewn using old T-shirts among their other handmade products. Who would want a quilt made from T-shirts? One big market has been parents of high-school and college seniors getting ready to graduate who send in the graduate's old T-shirts. The resulting quilt is a keepsake gift to treasure for a lifetime. Source: Yahoo Lifestyle

---

How Much Will Shoppers Pay?

The question almost every new maker asks is "how much should I charge for my work?" For pricing, an even more important question is "how much will shoppers pay?"

You don't want to lose money by asking only enough to get back your costs when customers will gladly pay higher prices.

To find the average price buyers will pay for pieces like yours, there are ways to survey what is selling where and for how much. This can be an adventure of sorts, going online to browse Etsy or Handmade on Amazon, or visiting craft fairs and stores to scope out the marketplace.

The average market price for an item may be higher at one place than it is in a different market(s). For example, an upcycled knitted hat may sell on Etsy at one price, at craft fairs at a different price, and in stores for a higher price.

My introduction to pricing came without warning. I was taking my first practice scarf off the loom when a visitor was walking through the studio where I was working. She oohhed and aahhed over the piece.

I had become weary of looking at the scarf because it had taken so many hours to finish. But my new admirer loved it. She asked, "*how much do you want for it?*" It never occurred to me anyone would buy the thing. I was clueless of its value. Without thinking, I blurted out, "*how about $35?*" She jumped on it. In hindsight, my asking price was pitifully low. Since that first sale, I've sold similar pieces for $150.

📢 **MILLENNIALS WILLING TO PAY MORE FOR SUSTAINABLE**

Ninety percent of millennials are willing to pay more for products that contain environmentally friendly or sustainable ingredients. Source: Nielsen.com

---

What Does It Cost to Make an Item

Cost of goods is what you spend to produce products you sell. Cost of goods includes all material, labor, and overhead costs.

Material Costs

In an upcycled art business, most of your supplies may not cost money, but will take time for gathering, cleaning, and preparing before assembling.

Besides raw materials, you may need accessories like thread, glue, paint, or others. Regardless of how little you use, include the costs of everything that goes into making each piece. Don't neglect to add any shipping charges and sales tax you paid for materials shipped to you.

As an example, say you make a lamp using mostly upcycled materials:

> Cost of materials from trash (not counting preparation): $0
> Glue, (lead-free) solder and miscellaneous supplies: $1.25
> Total materials cost: $1.25

Cost of Labor

Cost of labor is the dollar value of the time needed to gather, prepare and produce an item. If you make all your products yourself, your cost of labor would be the hourly wage you pay yourself or others you hire.

When starting out, make a few pieces first to learn realistically just how many hours you (or your workers) take to complete an item. Once you are up to what will be your average working speed, clock yourself making a single item.

How much is your time worth? This is something you have to decide, but a good starting amount is $20 per hour.

If you can sell items at a price that would pay you $30, $35, or more per hour, you can profitably hire others at a lower rate (like $15 per hour) to help produce your pieces when sales justify outsourcing labor.

Continuing with the example of the lamp made from upcycled materials, let's say you decided that you value your labor at $20 per hour.

> Time needed to collect, clean and prepare raw materials: 1 hour
> Time to assemble/complete lamp: 1 1/2 hours
> Total cost of labor: 2 1/2 hours x $20 per hour = $50

At this point you have calculated the cost of materials for the lamp at $1.25 and the labor at $50, bringing your costs so far to $51.25. We now need to account for another, often overlooked cost of doing business commonly known as overhead.

Overhead

Overhead refers to expenses you pay to operate a business day-to-day. Since most side hustles start from home, you don't need to worry about overhead. If you grow to the point of renting a space, then you have to pay attention.

Examples of overhead include: business licenses, rent, utilities, phone, insurance, advertising, bank charges, office supplies, cleaning supplies, and so on.

Calculating all those costs take time. An easy shortcut for a home business is to figure 25 percent of the total of your materials and labor costs to arrive at a number that approximates your overhead.

THE PRICING FORMULA

Using the lamp example:

Estimated overhead costs:
$50 labor + $1.25 materials = $51.25
$51.25 x 25% estimated overhead = $12.81

Total production cost for lamp:
$51.25 + $12.81 = $64.06

As you see in the example above, the total of labor, materials and overhead for making one lamp is $64.06. This is the amount we have to recover to break even.

But $64.06 isn't necessarily what you would price the lamp at.

Go back to the research you did earlier to learn the average market price for similar lamps. You may find lamps like yours sell on Etsy or Amazon or at crafts fairs for an average price of $100 or more. Since that's a price which shoppers are used to seeing, you would be in line to price yours at least $100 in those markets. If your asking price was $64.06, you would lose money.

Wholesale Pricing

Let's say handmade lamps like you make sell in stores for $200. You could set a wholesale price at $75. You will recover a little more than your costs, get paid what your time is worth, and make a profit.

Now what if your research showed the average price for lamps like yours was only $59. Since your production cost was $64.06, you would lose money trying to price at the market average. In a case like this, one needs to:
- Lower material or labor costs
- Enhance the perceived value of the lamps (see later in this chapter)
- Choose other, more profitable items to make.

📣 **TEENS PUT ON RECYCLED FASHION SHOW TO HELP AT-RISK YOUTH**

Young at Art Museum in Davie, FL has hosted an annual Recycled Fashion Show for over twelve years. Inspired and creative teens from the museum's Volunteer Program team up to create wearable fashion made from recycled materials like plastic, fabric remnants, newspaper, cardboard, and even bottle caps. Proceeds from the fashion show go to Young at Art's outreach assistance for at-risk youth in the area.

YOUR PROFIT MARGIN

One of the most important things to learn early on in your side hustle is your profit margin. This amount is the difference between your cost of goods and your asking price. Your profit margin will differ depending on whether you sell retail or wholesale.

If your cost of goods is $10 and your retail price is $30, your profit margin is $20. If your cost of goods is $10 and your wholesale price is $14, your profit margin is $4.

If doing the math gives you a headache, check out the free Craftmarketer.com/pricing-calculator/ to determine your profit margins and prices.

Knowing profit margins enables you to make choices for growth by telling you:

- How much money you can spend on ads.
- If you can afford to offer free shipping, which will increase your sales.
- If you can afford to hire help with production, which allows you to produce more inventory.
- If you can profitably sell wholesale to stores.

PRICING ONE-OF-A-KIND ITEMS

As a maker, you may be inspired to create large, artistic pieces like wall art or sculpture. If so, you are an artist. A gallery owner can help you determine a selling price after seeing your work.

Another example, someone at an art show sees your work and wants to commission you to do a custom piece. You can estimate prices by the square foot or cubic foot.

I made woven wall screens and I wanted to know how to quote prices for making screens according to whatever my customer needed. The customer may want a 4' x 8' screen, 2' x 5' or some other size.

I use salt cedar cuttings to make the screens because the color resembles mahogany. Salt cedar is an unwanted invader crop in New Mexico and Arizona. I can go to many areas and cut as much as I want for free.

It takes me an average of 15 minutes to gather and transport enough stalks to make one 3' x 6' screen. Between the gathering and the weaving, it takes 75 minutes to make a screen. That comes to $37.50 in labor costs.

I also have about $2 in yarn costs for warp and hem. Adding labor and materials, I am now up to $39.50 in costs. I multiply $39.50 x 25% to cover overhead and get $9.88. The total production cost of one of my screens is:

Materials: $2
Labor: $37.50
Overhead: $9.88
Total: $49.38

Next, I double my costs of goods as if I were a store buying from a supplier. This is a good way to ensure I make a healthy profit:

$$\$49.38 \times 2 = \$98.76$$

I want to come up with a reliable "per square foot price" I can give a customer that is asking about a custom-sized piece.

The square footage of my finished 3' x 6' screen comes to 18 square feet. I divide the amount I arrived at above by the square footage:

$$\$98.76 \div 18 = \$5.49$$

I know from my market research that $5.49 per square foot is too low. I can easily ask and get $10 per square foot when quoting a custom order.

Because I did the math, I also know there is enough profit margin to pay an interior designer a commission, should they sell one of my screens to a client of theirs for $10 - $11 per square foot.

For artists making larger pieces, you may not need to calculate a price-per-square-feet or cubic feet. With reputation comes a higher value. Grants for art in public places can earn artists anywhere from $1,000 to $100,000+ for a single piece. See the appendices for more on public art programs.

In a gallery where my scarves were retailing for $34, there were also $2,000 pieces made by a well-known fiber artist. She creates large tapestry pieces charging $100 per square foot to corporate clients. At this point in her career, she commands top dollar. As your own reputation grows, you also can raise your prices.

LOWER YOUR PRODUCTION COSTS

The more things you make, the more tips and tweaks you learn to speed the production time.

I have been a weaver and fiber artist for many years. Even so, I use Google to search for production tips. I found a list of 100 ways to weave better and faster. These tips saved me several minutes here and there in various stages of production. That may not sound like much, but every minute you can save and still produce quality finished products, the higher your profit margins.

Search Google for "_____ production tips," filling in the blank with your craft: sewing, knitting, woodworking, stained glass or another.

> 📢 **DOLLAR VALUES OF REPURPOSING**
>
> "A bar of iron costs $5 — made into horseshoes its worth is $12 — made into needles its worth is $3500 — made into balance springs for watches, its worth is $300,000. Your own value is determined also by what you are able to make of yourself." ~ Source Unknown

You have set up your new business, prepared your marketing materials and calculated prices. You are ready to let the world know about your upcycled crafts. There are so many opportunities to market your handmade items, it may be overwhelming. Don't feel you have to take them all at once. The next chapter shows how to schedule action steps, clarifying what to do and when to do it.

> **MORE UPCYCLE PRODUCT IDEAS:**
>
> - Make jewelry rings from old forks or spoons with patterned handles. Cut off handle and sand to smooth. Using a couple of needlenose pliers, bend the remaining metal to shape into a ring.
> - Upcycle plastic bags by winding different colored bags around plain bangle bracelets.
> - Make floor rugs using plastic grocery bags of different colors.
> - Another use for used plastic bags: woven flower pots.

CHAPTER 6

Your Marketing Plan

With so many possible actions you can take, it helps to map out your promotional actions day by day. A daily planner can serve as a low-cost marketing calendar. With a schedule, you never have to wonder what to do next.

To clear up any confusion about what marketing is, marketing is every communication you make about your product, yourself, or your side hustle.

It's how you describe what you do, how you dress, your business card, your product packaging, the colors you choose for your logo, and a lot more.

Marketing is often mistaken for advertising. Though advertising is a marketing tactic, it is only one of many. Not all marketing costs money.

To schedule your marketing communications, you need a list of actions to take. Start with the 101 possibilities extracted from this book.

They won't all be appropriate for you, but circle those that are so you can add them to your calendar. You will develop your own ideas as you grow in experience. Add your tactics to the list and to a daily planner (find many varieties on Amazon.)

101 Marketing-Related Actions

The following *Marketing Blueprint* of actions grouped by topics is available as a checklist. Ideas are explained throughout the chapters. Download the *Blueprint* at: Craftmarketer.com/book-resources/

SELL ARTS & CRAFTS FROM UPCYCLED MATERIALS

MAKING PRODUCTS
- [ ] Research products in demand
- [ ] Make quality products
- [ ] Design using colors that sell
- [ ] Create products using themes
- [ ] Personalize products
- [ ] Promote your sustainability
- [ ] Use recycled packaging material

PHOTOS & VIDEOS
- [ ] Take lots of attractive photos
- [ ] Product images with white background
- [ ] How-it's-made images & videos
- [ ] How-it's-used images & videos
- [ ] Lifestyle images
- [ ] Jury images for art & craft shows
- [ ] Headshot images of you
- [ ] Behind-the-scenes videos

BIZ STARTUP
- [ ] Choose a catchy business name
- [ ] Register for a business license
- [ ] Get set up to accept credit cards
- [ ] Set up accounting system

PRE-MARKETING
- [ ] Find your authentic voice
- [ ] Write your story
- [ ] Design logo
- [ ] Elevator pitch
- [ ] Choose your fonts and colors
- [ ] Add your contact info
- [ ] Business cards
- [ ] Hangtags
- [ ] Thank-you cards
- [ ] Signs and banners for events
- [ ] Postcards
- [ ] Certificates of authenticity
- [ ] Voice mail message
- [ ] Branding on all stationery

PRICING
- [ ] Average prices for similar work?
- [ ] Your production cost
- [ ] Your profit margin
- [ ] Can you lower your costs?

CROWDFUNDING
- [ ] Turn your story into a video
- [ ] Create a campaign on Indiegogo, Patreon or Kickstarter

SELL AT EVENTS
- [ ] Research art-craft shows, events
- [ ] Apply to shows
- [ ] Build attractive display
- [ ] Get pop-up tent
- [ ] Make a checklist for doing shows

SEO - SEARCH ENGINE OPTIMIZATION
- [ ] Use EtsyRank: find keywords
- [ ] Use keywords in social posts
- [ ] Use keywords in product listings
- [ ] Get inbound links

SELL ON ETSY
- [ ] Set up new Etsy shop, or
- [ ] Get critique of Etsy shop
- [ ] List products
- [ ] Keywords in title, tags, descriptions
- [ ] Add 10 images per listing
- [ ] Connect Etsy to social media
- [ ] Test Etsy Promoted Listings
- [ ] Increase number of listings
- [ ] Market Etsy store offline
- [ ] Offer free shipping if possible

ALTERNATIVES TO ETSY
- [ ] List on Amazon Handmade
- [ ] List on other Etsy alternatives
- [ ] Set up your own domain site
- [ ] Wordpress plugin for Etsy Store
- [ ] Test ads on social media sites

BLOGGING
- [ ] Set up blog about your niche
- [ ] Optimize blog posts for SEO
- [ ] Syndicate posts to social media

SOCIAL MEDIA
- [ ] Post at least once a day or more
- [ ] Post with video for engagement
- [ ] Posts: educate, entertain, inspire
- [ ] Post links to your products
- [ ] Schedule posting using apps
- [ ] Research popular hashtags
- [ ] Post on Facebook
- [ ] Post to Instagram
- [ ] Tweet to Twitter
- [ ] Pin to Pinterest boards
- [ ] Get social followers' e-mails

SELL ARTS & CRAFTS FROM UPCYCLED MATERIALS

SELL WHOLESALE
- [ ] Determine production capacity
- [ ] Costs = 25% or less of the retail price
- [ ] Professional presentation
- [ ] Find store buyers using LinkedIn
- [ ] List on Faire, Tundra, Indieme, WholesaleInABox
- [ ] Offer online ordering for stores
- [ ] Sell on consignment
- [ ] Approach restaurants, gift stores
- [ ] Place upcycled art in galleries

PUBLIC ART PROGRAMS
- [ ] Research public art programs
- [ ] Apply to public art grants

FREE PUBLICITY
- [ ] Prepare online media kit
- [ ] Identify influencers with Heepsy
- [ ] Use Twitter to find reporters
- [ ] USNPL lists newspaper writers
- [ ] Create brief pitch to media
- [ ] Link to full press release

CUSTOMER MAILING LIST
- [ ] Set up e-mail management app like Aweber or Mailchimp
- [ ] Ask customers to give e-mail
- [ ] Schedule follow-up calendar

MISCELLANEOUS
- [ ] Track and measure all actions
- [ ] Listen to what shoppers tell you
- [ ] Answer all inquiries quickly
- [ ] Personalize communications
- [ ] Treat customers fabulously
- [ ] Make stuff you love making

📣 **LAND OF PHAROAHS REWARDS ENVIRONMENTAL ART**

Working to increase children's awareness of environmental protection, Egypt launched the Best Environmental Artistic Awards for students of all ages. Students participate in the competition by submitting their aesthetic paintings, made from recycled raw materials like paper and cans. Winners receive financial awards. Source: EgyptToday.com.

Daily Planner / Marketing Calendar

After you identify which action steps you want to work with, use a planner / calendar to organize and schedule them. A planner protects you from getting lost by mapping a direction and a timeline. It shows you the big picture.

Your planner helps you avoid costly shotgun marketing and engage in laser-focused, profitable actions you can track and measure. The following is an example of a daily page from a marketing calendar.

Date:			
Action	Cost	To Do	Result
take product and artist photos	none: DIY	set up lightbox and lighting	good for Etsy listings, but need more for social posting
write my artist story	none: DIY	set aside time to write story of how I came to make upcycled art	add my image and post to online store
research local craft shows	none: DIY	create account at zapplication.org. look for well-attended shows within a day's drive	found 2 events
get critique of Etsy shop	$15 at fiverr.com	sign in to fiverr and contact Etsy store reviewer for details. order critique	critique revealed several areas I can improve my Etsy shop
discover profit margin for item I'm thinking to wholesale	none: DIY	add up material, labor and overhead. use online pricing calculator	retail is $30, cost is $20. margin too low to wholesale this item
design and order hangtags	$20 at Vistaprint	design hangtags using Photoshop or Gimp	hangtags added to each item.
post Facebook video of me making new item	none: DIY	set up lighting in work area. record video of production process. edit with Camtasia.	posted video to Facebook resulting in 28 likes, 2 shares and 1 sale

Now that you have a plan and a calendar of steps to take, you may be wondering how you will generate cash to get started or grow. Consider crowdfunding. You are about to learn how creative upcyclers have raised money from generous supporters.

> 📣 **CRAFTING RECYCLED PLASTIC BAGS**
>
> Plarn (plastic yarn) is made from cutting strips of plastic shopping bags. Lay out the bags flat. Cut off handles to make edges straight. Wearing gloves, use rubbing alcohol to get rid of printing. Apply your own colors with magic marker pens. Cut bags into strips. (See videos at Craftmarketer.com/tutorials for hundreds of how-tos.) Use the resulting material for knitting or crocheting or weaving products to resell like: baskets, floor mats, outdoor furniture covering, wall art, lamp shades, bracelets, plastic flowers, backpacks, dog leashes, tote-bags, and purses.

> **MORE UPCYCLE PRODUCT IDEAS:**
>
> - Upcycle an old sweater into a cool looking lampshade.
> - Turn old furniture hardware, like handles, into necklaces.
> - Reverse the above: take old necklace centerpieces and use as furniture handles.
> - Upcycle an old scarf into a wreath.
> - Blend scraps of paper, water, and wildflower seeds and shape into balls. After dried, they can be thrown into the ground. Rain and sun will do the rest.

CHAPTER 7

Crowdfunding

Money to start and keep your business growing could come from several sources. Borrowing on your credit cards or tapping your savings may seem like easy choices. Another option that's worked for many is using other people's money through crowdfunding.

Crowdfunding is an online way of raising money where the public makes donations or sometimes advance purchases to a cause or business.

An individual or group appeals for funds using a compelling video and written story about what they do and why they need more money to start or complete their project. Many startups offer donors a product or discount as an incentive to make donations.

Popular crowdfunding sites used by artists, artisans, and pro-environment causes to get money for their projects include:
- Indiegogo.com
- Kickstarter.com
- Crowdfunder.com
- Gofundme.com
- StartSomeGood.com
- Patreon.com/explore/diy

> 📣 **ART MADE FROM RECYCLING VINYL RECORDS**
>
> Shawn McClure's Skylinyl company cuts detailed images into recycled vinyl records. His IndieGogo campaign brought in $77,776 and has been seen on TechCrunch, CNN, GeekWire, and more.

Successful crowdfunding campaigns work because the producer marketed the campaign outside the crowdfunding platform, drove traffic to their campaign, and combined emotional triggers in their story that motivated donors.

Tips for creating a crowdfunding campaign:

- ☐ Answer this question first: why should a person care about your project? If you aren't clear, your message won't convert.
- ☐ Define your avatar or perfect donor so you can find where they spend time online, monitor their social posts, and learn to use the same language they use.
- ☐ Plan a marketing campaign to get your message out. Crowdfunding sites don't drum up donors for you, though if you get enough contributions from your own efforts, your video could go viral.
- ☐ Be yourself. Being authentic is magnetic. Corporations don't have a soul, but you do.
- ☐ People love stories. Facts tell, but stories sell, especially those that evoke emotions.
- ☐ Tell people why you are doing what you're doing. Studies prove that adding the word *because* when asking for action increases response.
- ☐ Got reviews or kudos for your previous work? What others say about you (social proof) is more convincing than what you say about you.
- ☐ Point out a common enemy. Example: manufacturers pollute the environment. People join your cause to help you fight the bad guys.
- ☐ Show your product and how you create it.
- ☐ People are skeptical. If you make claims, provide evidence.
- ☐ If your campaign is reward-based, point out what donors receive.

- [ ] If your budget allows, send a news release out to the media announcing your crowdfunding project. Combining crowdfunding with publicity leverages your reach. For tips on writing a news release about your project, see blog.fundly.com/crowdfunding-press-release/.

- [ ] Study the video pitches of other successful campaigns. Search the big crowdfunding sites for "recycled" or "upcycled" noting campaigns that got funded. You'll find they use many of the triggers in the above list.

Crowdfunding isn't for everyone. It takes a lot of preparation and work to pull off a winning campaign. If it doesn't generate cash, you may feel you've wasted your time.

Win or lose, putting together a crowdfunding campaign will teach you a lot about how to define your mission and your message online. Offline, displaying your repurposed art and crafts at events is probably the fastest way to discover if shoppers will buy your items.

```
                MORE UPCYCLE PRODUCT IDEAS:

    •   Apply a variety of vintage jewelry using
        glue around old mirror frames.
    •   Make necklaces and bracelets from old
        scrabble tiles by drilling small holes in
        the tiles and stringing together.
    •   Using an old bike tire inner tube, trace and
        cut out a feather shape. Using scissors,
        cut fine lines partially here and there to
        duplicate the look of real feathers. Attach
        to old earring clasps.
```

CHAPTER 8

Selling at Art and Craft Shows and Other Events

A rt and craft fairs, festivals, and consumer expos attract thousands of shoppers who buy handmade and upcycled items.

Art and craft shows are a great venue for testing your products to learn how shoppers react. Even better, events can put cash in your wallet immediately.

Shows and events don't require a huge commitment. You can do one or two events, feel the pulse of the market for your product line, and then go on to other events.

Selling at shows has challenges. Events can be physically and energetically taxing. At a busy show, you may talk to hundreds of shoppers about your products and your process.

With so many events happening year-round, it's important to choose the right ones for your work. The better-attended shows require vendors pay for booth rental fees six months or longer in advance of the event. The top shows are highly competitive because they historically perform well for sellers.

Discover if selling at fairs and events is for you. Here we cover:
- Types of events
- How to find events
- How much shows cost you
- How much can you earn
- How to apply
- Displaying your products
- Accepting credit cards
- Checklist for preparing
- More tips for having great shows

TYPES OF EVENTS

Events and shows that hand-makers display their work at include:

Art and craft shows. Art and craft shows can be juried, or not. Juried means you apply with images of your work and judges decide to accept or reject your application. Jurying (ideally) weeds out vendors selling imported products that are not handmade.

Juried shows are often annual events, with a history of good attendance. Examples of annual juried art and craft shows that draw hundreds of thousands of visitors include: Plaza Art Fair in Kansas City; Rio Grande Arts and Crafts Fair Balloon Festival in Albuquerque; One-of-a-Kind Holiday Show in Chicago; Tempe Festival of the Arts in the Phoenix area; and Bayou City Art Festival in Houston.

Recycled art shows. Many high schools put on recycled art and craft shows. Getting a booth here is your best starting point. Note that your recycled art may stand out from the crowd in the more general art and craft shows mentioned above.

Popular recycled art events for the public include: Recycled Arts Festival in Esther Short Park, Vancouver, WA; McMinnville Recycled Arts Festival in Oregon; Déjà Vu Art and Fine Craft Show in Columbus, Indiana; and the Seattle Recycled Arts Festival in Washington.

📣 **THE TRASH SHOW: HAWAII ARTISTS RECYCLE**

Ira Ono, known for his recycled art and jewelry, started "Hawaii Artists Recycle" back in 1988 to provide an opportunity for local artists to display their pieces made from recycled materials. "The Trash Show: Hawaii Artists Recycle" is among the longest-running annual arts events in Hawaii and the US. Source: BigIslandNow.com

---

Renaissance fairs. These outdoor events include vendors of arts and crafts booths as a part of a total entertainment package featuring a medieval theme.

A variety of food, drink, jugglers, jousters, knights and fair maidens abound at these festivals. Some popular renaissance shows run each weekend from one to two months. Vendors commit to a long-term booth and decorate with a medieval theme.

Examples: Arizona Renaissance Festival held weekends from early February to late March in Gold Canyon, AZ; Sherwood Forest Faire held from early February to early March in McDade, TX; Florida Renaissance Festival in February and March in Deerfield Beach, FL; and Minnesota Renaissance Festival held weekends from mid-August until end-September in Shakopee, MN.

Farmer's markets. In most cities of any size, you can find farmer's markets with local growers showing their produce when in season. Many farmer's markets also allow locally-made handcrafted products.

Flea markets. If you make low-priced items, consider setting up at a popular flea market if there's one local to you. One of the most well-known is *First Monday* in Canton, Texas, attracting over 250,000 visitors each month.

📣 **FROM SCRAP YARD TO ART**

The City of Santa Cruz, CA puts on an annual exhibit of the Santa Cruz Recycled Art Program (SCRAP). The show features creative artwork made from upcycled and repurposed materials gathered from the city's scrap yard.

BE WARY OF....

After years of displaying at different events, both winners and losers, I urge caution when considering:

First-time events. Avoid events that are new. First-time shows have not built a following so attendance can be poor to non-existent.

Be highly suspicious of show promoters who approach you at a show attempting to sell you on applying to *their* upcoming event. They will tell you how great their show is and how their vendors are all happy with their sales. *Reality check*. If their show was as good as they make it out to be, they wouldn't need to look for vendors. The better shows always get more applicants than there are available booth spaces.

Shows another vendor did well at. You may get excited hearing the advice of other sellers who recommend an event. Be cautious, though. I've gone into shows after someone told me how great it was for them. Yet, in many of these instances my work didn't sell enough to make me want to go back the next year. I've also done super at some events that other vendors tell me they'll never do again.

In most big cities, you will see ads for **expos for selling products** like local fashion shows, home and garden shows, pet shows, and many others. Unless an event targets a *sustainable-conscious* or *buy handmade* audience, attendees may ignore your display completely. As with any event, visit the show before you commit and take notes on which booths are busy with visitors.

Music festivals attract a party crowd that likes to drink, eat junk food, and listen to live bands. Nothing wrong with music festivals if you want a good time, but the crowd isn't there shopping for higher-priced handmade products. If you sell a low-priced item, music events may work for you.

Finding Events

How do you find the good art and craft shows, festivals and expos where you can expect decent sales? Find events in the US and Canada (sometimes with vendor reviews) at:
zapplication.org
art-linx.com
artfaircalendar.com
festivalnet.com
To locate shows internationally, see Appendix 2.

Announcements of shows also appear in magazines and websites for different craft media. *Sunshine Artist* and *Handmade Business* list shows, sales and attendance figures of the bigger art and craft shows.

Another source of art and craft shows will be your state arts council. Find an agency near you at: Arts.gov/partners/state-regional

Questions to Answer Before Applying for Events

- [ ] Is the show well known? How many years has it been held? Does the promoter advertise in the news-papers, on radio, billboards, or TV? The public knows about the popular events and returns faithfully to see what's new.

- [ ] How many booth spaces are available for the whole show? A show with 500 booths will draw bigger crowds than a show with only fifty.

- [ ] What is the booth rental fee? Is there an extra fee for corner spaces? Usually, there is because corners are better selling locations.

- [ ] Is there a jury fee? Popular shows charge a separate fee just for applying. The application fee isn't returned if you are rejected, nor is it deducted from your booth fee if you are accepted.

- [ ] What size spaces are available? The typical size is 10' x 10' and that is the most common pop-up canopy tent size available.

- [ ] Is the event restricted to handmade items?

- [ ] Is the show outdoors or inside? If outdoors, what has the weather historically been like at that time of year.

- [ ] If the show is outdoors, is it held on streets, sidewalks, parking lots, or grassy area? Most streets are not level, requiring you to adjust your booth display.

- [ ] What are the hours of the event? Most shows require someone to be in your booth throughout the show hours.

- [ ] Is setup allowed the day before? If you get into a show where this is the case, take advantage of it.

- [ ] How is vendor loading and unloading organized?
- [ ] How far away is vendor parking?
- [ ] What are the security arrangements? Well-organized outdoor events provide security overnight. When you purchase your pop-up tent, get one with side panels so you can zip up the walls.

> 📢 **OLD CITY MARKET ATTRACTS SUSTAINABLE ART**
>
> Old City Knoxville is home to The Old City Market. Many of the artisans exhibiting their art and crafts make their work using low-waste and ethical sources. Though the market isn't promoted as an "eco-friendly" fair, a lot of the vendors use recycled materials, which is a big draw. Source: UTDailyBeacon.com

What Shows Cost

Art and craft show expenses include:
- Jury application fees for the more competitive events (non-refundable even if you are not accepted)
- Booth space rental (usually 10' x 10')
- Travel costs: gas, motel, meals, parking fees
- Your display (grid walls or artist pro-panels, tables)
- Pop-up canopy with side walls
- Weights (to keep your tent from blowing away)
- Also, see the checklist for craft shows later in this chapter

Vendor rental fees at art and craft shows range from $25 a day to $1,000 for a weekend. Local events, like those sponsored by a high school, church or community center, can be inexpensive and easier to get accepted in. Small local events will cost less because you won't have to spend money on travel.

Big-city, popular juried shows charge higher booth-rental fees. They get more applicants than there are available spaces. The sales potential of well-attended shows can be good (but not guaranteed) so traveling to a neighboring state may be worth the added costs.

How Much Can You Earn

It's almost impossible to estimate your potential earnings from shows without doing them and measuring the results for yourself.

I've been in shows where I sold nothing. When this happens, I don't go back the next year.

On the other end of the spectrum, one event brought in over $10,000 in sales over a three-day period. I have returned to the show year after year with good results, but did not reach that level again. (I originally found the event by Googling "top craft shows in the US").

Other sellers I met at different shows told me they did not do well at my best event and will never return. If I had talked to them before I experienced my fantastic weekend, I might never have tried it.

I spoke with an artist who only applies to events where he can average sales higher than 10K per weekend. He loads his work into his RV and travels a circuit of shows around the country.

I don't average 10K per show, because it would mean being on the road between distant cities for much of the year. Instead, I opt for shows that bring in less money but are easier and cheaper to get attend.

However, you cannot rely on what I or other vendors tell you about their earnings from shows. Their success doesn't prove the same event will do well for your product line. Sure, it's an indicator, but you can only really know from doing the show yourself. Walk through a show you think might be good for your work and observe how busy the other vendors are. If they are actively selling, then consider applying for the event the next year and testing it.

How to Apply

Most shows and fairs require vendors to fill out an application, either online or via a mailed-in form. <u>Zapplication.org</u> lets you apply to and pay for multiple shows from one website. For the more competitive shows, vendor applications are often due six months to a year before the actual show date.

Jury Images

If applying for the more competitive events, it may be worth the investment to hire a photographer experienced in art or craft images for juried shows. If you can't afford a photographer and have to take your own photos, see the examples at: http://bermangraphics.com/digital-jury-resources/fixing-jury-images.htm

Booth Location

You can't always choose your booth location, but when possible, take advantage of the opportunity. If you have exhibited at an event in the past, managers may give you the same location you had before, or at least give your booth preference a higher priority.

Corner locations (extra fee) can be better, because they allow you to open up to traffic flow from two sides.

Getting a booth space near a main walkway close to the show's main entrance will probably be a better location than at the back of the event. Though at well-attended shows, there are no bad locations.

Avoid getting a space near food vendors or entertainment. Food is the top seller at shows and not only are you competing for attention, you must deal with junk food being carried in and around your work. Noise from the entertainment can prevent you from being able to talk to your customers pleasantly.

If you don't like your allotted space, ask the show manager before you set up if you can move.

DISPLAYING YOUR PRODUCTS

Your booth should be inviting for customers to walk in and look around. Build your display at home first, and play with variations of how the arrangement looks with your pieces displayed.

Design the layout of your booth to be flexible. Build it so you can set up at least two ways:

1. First arrangement for a booth location within a row of booths, set up with three side walls and opening in front for visitors to enter.

2. Second arrangement for corner location has two side walls in back and two open sides for visitor traffic coming from two directions.

There are lots of possibilities for setting up your display. I rearranged my display from show to show until I came up with a display that worked best for attracting shoppers.

For ideas for booth displays, see:

- pinterest.com/lifethriftylane/craft-show-display-ideas/
- pinterest.com/junqdiva/diy-craft-show-display-and-set-up-ideas/
- pinterest.com/dillydally/craft-show-booth-inspiration/

A general rule in retail: *the fuller your display, the more you will sell.* Studies show shoppers buy more from a full rack or table.

Keep your display racks and tables neat during the entire show. It may mean going over to straighten merchandise many times during the day.

Fixtures and Lighting

Fixtures, racks, grids, pillars and tables allow you to hang or place your products. Find cheap used fixtures from stores going out of business who advertise on eBay, Craigslist or Facebook Marketplace.

When doing indoor events, use track lighting running above your display to direct spotlights on your pieces.

Pop Up Canopy Tent

For outdoor events, you need protection from sun and weather. A pop-up canopy will adequately protect you and your pieces. Physical safety of your customers, fellow vendors, and your merchandise must be a priority in constructing your booth. Frame and covers should be sturdy enough to withstand high winds, rain, and large crowds.

Bring weights to attach to your pop-up tent. Weights keep your tent from blowing into your neighbor's display.

White tarps work best with pop-up tents. Colored tarps cast a hue on your merchandise.

Get a pop-up tent you can quickly set up and easily break down for transport. You want to be able to quickly set up your tent and break it down at the end of the event.

KD canopy and EZ Up have been making pop-up tents for art and craft fairs for many years. Check Craigslist or eBay for deals. Search for "canopy tent" or "EZ up tent" or "pop-up tent".

Accept Credit Cards

As described earlier, being able to accept credit cards will help your sales, especially at art and craft shows. Mobile phone card readers make it easy to process sales quickly. Refer to Chapter 3 for providers. Credit card purchases can increase your overall sales by 30% to 40%.

📣 **EMERALD ISLE ENCOURAGES TRASHY FASHION**

Junk Kouture is a fashion competition which challenges young people to design and create 100%-recycled couture from everyday junk. Junk Kouture is open to students in the Republic of Ireland, Northern Ireland, and Scotland. The competition combines fashion, design, and environmental sustainability and transforms them into a contest that has attracted 100,000 audience members. Source: JunkKouture.com

---

CHECKLIST FOR WHAT TO TAKE TO SHOWS

Getting ready for a show is exciting. But you don't want to get so carried away you forget something important. A checklist is helpful when getting ready for a show. Depending on what you make, your list may differ, but here is a suggested one you can adjust to your own needs.

- ☐ Pop-up tent with canopy top and sidewalls for zipping up tent overnight
- ☐ Weights to hold down the tent in heavy wind gusts
- ☐ Gridwalls or pro-panels for walls
- ☐ Display tables and chairs
- ☐ Small folding table to make sales transactions. This will be where the customer can comfortably write a check or sign for a credit card sale.
- ☐ Skirting for tables
- ☐ Mirror (if you sell wearables)
- ☐ Dolly for moving your display and merchandise back and forth from your vehicle
- ☐ Food, snacks, and water—though popular events often have food vendors
- ☐ Branded recycled shopping bags with your website URL
- ☐ Business cards with URL for your Etsy or online store
- ☐ Fanny pack or similar to hold change; bring about $100 in ones and fives. DO NOT use a cash box as it is a visual target for thieves
- ☐ Receipt book for those who want a written receipt.
- ☐ Sales report form - helps you track sales and expenses for each event: record mileage from home, which items sell, hotel, food, parking, etc.
- ☐ Mailing list form or ledger – collect e-mails by offering a giveaway item contest
- ☐ Credit card reader: Square, PayPal, or other form of credit card reader that plugs into your smartphone; take an extra card reader as backup
- ☐ Small USB battery charger for your mobile phone

- [ ] Consider getting a mobile hot spot device for your phone in areas where there is no Wifi
- [ ] Dress in layers. It can be cold in mornings when setting up and hot by noon
- [ ] Battery-operated fan for hot days
- [ ] Power strip, extension cords, lighting for indoor events
- [ ] Paper towels, toilet paper, and handy wipes
- [ ] Tool box with: extra pens, notepad, scissors, needle, thread, crochet hook, tape (scotch and duct), roll of velcro, push pins or thumbtacks, extra pins, screwdrivers, pliers, heavy string or twine, zip ties, bungee cords
- [ ] Insect repellent, sunscreen
- [ ] Sun hat, sunglasses
- [ ] Signs, banners, or large posters with your biz name and models of your product in lifestyle setting
- [ ] Sales tax permit
- [ ] Local business license (if required)

Download the *Checklist for What to Take to Craft Shows* at: Craftmarketer.com/book-resources/

More Tips for Successful Shows

- [ ] Show up to events early. You never know how setup will go, with many vendors arriving at the same time—all in a hurry to get their displays up.
- [ ] Make it easy for customers to buy. Have all the materials you need to complete a sale nearby, including: receipt book, brochures, business cards, price lists, and bags or boxes for packaging sales.

- [ ] Have a receipt book for customers who want a written receipt. It also makes a great excuse to get the customer's address.

- [ ] Ask customers to get on your mailing list. If they don't buy at the show, they may purchase your work later.

- [ ] Have a supply of artist statements, bookmarks, business cards or postcards about you and your work to give with each sale or inquiry.

- [ ] For indoor events, consider buying a carpet remnant or rug for your booth. It looks good and gives you and your customers some relief from concrete floors.

- [ ] Make price signs or price tags. You will tire of answering the question: "how much is it?"

- [ ] For makers of wearables, wear something you have made; be a walking ad for your work.

- [ ] If you have won competitions, post your awards.

- [ ] Bring your own food. It lessens your time away from your booth during the busy part of the day.

- [ ] Keep notes about shows by name, city, travel distance, costs, crowd size, weather, parking, layout, sales, and other notes to yourself.

- [ ] Shows can be both exciting and demanding. Hundreds, possibly thousands of potential customers come by your booth, many of whom will look at your work and talk to you briefly. It helps if a friend or family member can assist you. Setting up the booth and handling sales goes easier with two people. At some point, you will want to take a break, or walk around and see the other booths.

Events let you meet people, make sales, and add new names to your customer list. Not everyone will buy at an event, but they may take your card or agree to be on your mailing list.

> 📢 **JURIED CRAFT SHOWS INTRODUCED ME TO THE BEST BUYERS**
>
> I love getting accepted into competitive art and craft shows. The better shows draw big crowds. Many shoppers with a keen eye for well-made crafts come through ready to buy. Before I began making a scarf from recycled materials, I didn't know how the public would react. I liked them, but the only way to know if they would sell was to put them on display before lots of lookers. The show attendees not only liked the recycled scarves, they preferred them over all my others.

Though meeting customers at events is probably the fastest way to market your products—cool handmade stuff practically sells itself—you may prefer to stay home and sell online. The coming chapters give you tools and resources for growing an e-commerce side hustle. The first step is understanding SEO or *Search Engine Optimization* and you are about to learn how to use it to attract shoppers online searching for products like yours.

> **MORE UPCYCLE PRODUCT IDEAS:**
>
> Remix Plastic, started by Anthea Madill, is a New Zealand based company that sold over 3,500 recycled products in 2022. Among there products is a beautiful line of jewellry from sustainable or recycled materials. Pieces are constructed from local plastic waste diverted from landfills. Each item comes with a sustainability story that helps spread the message reduce, repurpose, reuse. See her product line at: https://remixplastic.com/

CHAPTER 9

SEO Tips

Search Engine Optimization

SEO–or search engine optimization–refers to using techniques to improve a web page's likelihood of showing up in search results for specific search terms or keywords.

If your product listing, blog post or YouTube video shows up on the first page for a search, it brings you free, organic traffic. There aren't many ways to market for free, but SEO is probably the closest to free you will find.

When you think of search engines, Google, Bing, or Yahoo may come to mind. But Etsy, Amazon, and eBay are also search engines, as well as shopping carts.

The factors that go into how e-commerce search engines rank one page over another for specific keyword searches change regularly. But there are elements that consistently influence search rankings you will discover in the following topics:

• Finding search terms buyers use
• Inbound links to your pages
• Engagement
• Where to place keywords and tags
• Keyword tools

Search is powerful. It has driven the boom of e-commerce both through mobile devices and computers. Eighty-seven percent of people using a smartphone search online at least once a day (source: SMAMarketing.net).

People search online for solutions to their problems. They search for opportunities. They search for entertainment. They search to learn. More important to you, they search for handmade and sustainable products to buy.

FINDING SEARCH TERMS BUYERS USE

You have probably come across the following words: tags, keywords, and search terms. For our purposes, they refer to the same thing. They are the words and phrases people type in a search bar to find what they need online.

In order for your product pages to show up in search results, you must include popular and relevant search terms used by shoppers. If you don't include popular search terms on your pages, your items won't get found.

Example of SEO

Because SEO is technical and often confusing, the simplest way to explain how SEO works is to show you an example. Let's say I make and sell jewelry from scrap materials. I might start off imagining my product listing needs to be found in online searches related to "recycled jewelry".

Typing in "recycled jewelry" at EtsyRank.com's keyword tool reveals other terms that can help increase traffic to my product pages. While 'recycled jewelry' got eleven searches in a recent month, other related search terms were more popular among searchers:

Search Term	Searches Per Month
recycled earrings	88
handmade earrings	19
upcycled earrings	17
boho earrings	14
repurposed earrings	11
recycled jewelry	11

The research provided me a list of more popular terms to include in my product listings, expanding my page's potential to get more visitors and buyers.

INBOUND LINKS TO YOUR PAGES

Using popular keywords is an important part of SEO for Etsy, Amazon, and other online stores. But there's another element that can affect your ranking in Google, Yahoo, and Bing search results—inbound links pointing to your product listing pages. An example of an inbound link: a blogger writes a review about one of your products and includes a link to your Etsy store.

Inbound links add authority to your page rankings because they are like votes coming in to tell the search engine that your page is relevant for the text in the link.

If you wanted to rank higher for "recycled vintage earrings" in Google searches, you would ask some sites to link to you with the link text reading <u>recycled vintage earrings</u>. Hidden from the viewer is the actual hyperlink that leads to your page.

But you have to be careful not to go overboard with getting a bunch of inbound links saying the same thing. Google sees this as spam. Instead, you want a variety of inbound link texts. Some inbound link texts could be your URL. Some could be the phrase for which you want to rank high. And others could be semantically-related phrases or your business name.

📢 **RECYCLED GROCERY BAGS FROM PET FOOD BAGS**

```
The phrase 'recycled grocery bags' was searched
for 800 times in a recent 30-days on Amazon
and 'reusable grocery bags' was searched for
2,240 times on Etsy. Nearly 5,700 Amazon buyers
searched for 'recycled tote bag.' Large size
farm feed and pet food bags are made from sturdy
material so they don't break. Most people toss
them in the trash when empty. But you can easily
convert them into tote bags and sell them
online. For a DIY video of how to make, see bit.
ly/recycledtotes. Etsy sellers are getting from
$8 to $12 per bag and some have sold hundreds.
```

ENGAGEMENT

Another factor that influences your SEO rankings is the amount and frequency of engagement your page receives from real people. For example, you post a video on your Facebook page with a link to your Etsy store. Your followers click through your link and check out your product pages. That engagement, including how much time a visitor spends, is tracked and measured by Google, which then becomes part of the algorithm that determines how Google will rank your landing page.

WHERE TO PLACE KEYWORDS AND TAGS

Placing popular tags in your Etsy, Amazon, and other online shop product listing pages increases your chances of getting found in search. There is a strategy to where you place keywords. Here are the areas to place your tags in your product listings for SEO purposes:

- [ ] Title: The first 40 characters (first few words) of your title are the most important for SEO, so include the most popular buyer keywords at the beginning.

- [ ] Description: Create a product description that promises benefits to the buyer. Insert popular keywords and tags throughout.

- [ ] Attributes: Attributes are extra tags like colors and materials. People search for "red" scarves or "cotton" clothing.

- [ ] "About" page: Your artist's story is an often-overlooked area to include your keywords. Weave them into your personal narrative.

- [ ] Shop announcement: Yet another area where you can include popular search terms.

- [ ] Tags: Use all allowable tags. They should differ from each other. Optimally, tags should match as many of the words in your product's title as possible.

- [ ] Categories: Categories act like tags. For instance, if you sell scarves under the category "Scarves" don't waste one of your tags with the word "scarves."

- [ ] Shop policies and terms. Include your popular search terms in your policies content. Most sellers neglect this area.

- [ ] One and two-word tags like "jewelry" or "handbag" are too broad for you to rank well for. Multi-word phrases are both easier to rank for and more likely to be used by someone ready to buy. For example, "tote bag" is a popular search term (over 90,000 searches on Google in a recent month) but not necessarily one used by shoppers alone. Whereas, "black tote bag" (8,100 searches in the same recent month) is more specific and probably used by those shopping for exactly that.

- [ ] Though your main keywords should be phrases used by buyers, there is an overall SEO benefit to including a mix of both broad and specific search terms in your product description.

Wordpress SEO

For bloggers using Wordpress, it may feel like too much trouble to keep up with SEO and provide content. Fortunately, there is an easy-to-use, free plugin called Yoast SEO. Yoast scans your posts and suggests how many keywords to use, where to place them, how long your content should be, the readability your content, and more SEO goodies.

📣 **GET MORE TRAFFIC TO YOUR WEBSITE. POST USEFUL TIPS.**

Get more visitors to your website by posting useful tips related to your products. For example, if you make scarves or shawls, write a post or create an infographic about how to wear your item. The phrase "how to wear scarf" was searched for over 18,000 times in January, 2020. "How to wear a shawl" wasn't as popular, but still got close to 2,000 searches. Stumped for ideas around your item? Check out AnswerThePublic.com. Type in "how to" and the search engine returns terms and phrases people are searching for starting with "how to."

Seasonal SEO

With a basic knowledge of SEO, you can take advantage of seasonal searches. For instance, shoppers search for "Christmas gifts for men" or "girlfriend gifts for Valentines" in the weeks and months leading up to those shopping times.

Change your tags on your product listings throughout the year to position your products for those special occasions. Start using seasonal tags at least two months in advance to give search engines like Google time to index your listings.

Keyword Tools

Etsy provides free "Search Analytics" for sellers with a sales history. This is invaluable if you have been on Etsy for at least a few months and made sales. You'll discover which keywords buyers used to find your product listing. To view, go to your Shop Manager > Marketing > Search analytics. We will go deeper into Etsy in the next chapter.

Etsyrank.com, SaleSamurai.io and Marmalead.com are subscription services that make keyword research easier for Etsy sellers. Serious Amazon Handmade sellers may want to consider subscribing to MerchantWords.com. Their tool gives search terms used by real buyers on Amazon.

Are these tools expensive? Subscription fees vary. If you can uncover new search terms that result in increased sales, it could be worth the investment, even if you only use the service for one month. You can export your research, save the search data files, and then cancel your subscription. Search terms are seasonal and can change over time, so come back to the tools every few months.

A note about using Google for research: other sellers use Google for competitive research. So if you use an SEO tool that tells you how many searches on Google were made for a particular phrase, know that those searchers aren't all buyers.

Whatever methods you play with for your keyword research, start off with a list of words and phrases you think best describe your items. Then, use the keyword tools to find related terms and phrases used by searchers.

Most services let you export your research results as a spreadsheet file, from which you can sort and arrange the results according to your needs.

SEO may seem intimidating, but even a little research can go a long way to uncovering keyword phrases shoppers are using every day to find handmade sustainable products like yours.

Keyword research can also help more people find your blog articles, your posts on Instagram, Pinterest, Facebook, Twitter, and your product listings on Etsy.

Selling on Etsy requires more than simply posting product listings and hoping buyers flock to your online shop. The next chapter prepares you for what you need to know to succeed on Etsy, THE online marketplace for consumers looking to *buy handmade.*

📢 THE IMPACT OF RECYCLING PLASTIC

Recycling plastics lowers the amount of resources (like: water, oil, natural gas, coal) used to manufacture plastic. According to one study, a pint-sized bottle of water takes almost 2,000 times the energy to get the same amount of tap water. Some landfill yards burn plastic bottles to save space. But doing so adds toxic pollutants into the air. (ThoughtCo.com)

CHAPTER 10

Selling On Etsy

Etsy has around 40 million active buyers browsing handmade products from almost two million sellers. Etsy buyers are loyal—81% are repeat customers who account for annual sales exceeding three billion dollars.

Etsy's primary market caters to the *buy handmade* audience. Many of these shoppers are also environmentally conscious.

As a selling platform, Etsy makes it easy to get started for new sellers to set up a shop and add product listings. If you aren't already a member, begin by registering for an account. Then click on "Sell on Etsy" to start.

The Etsy Seller Guide at etsy.com/seller-handbook will get you up and running using best practices from successful sellers.

YouTube.com offers hundreds of free tutorial videos on all aspects of setting up an Etsy store. Many of them will be trailers or lead magnets for paid courses. But you can get a lot of solid tips for free.

The best practices outlined in this chapter will help you set up your Etsy shop to succeed. Here you will learn about:
- Pre-setup steps
- Setting up your Etsy shop
- Product listings
- Images
- Etsy SEO
- Your product descriptions
- Share on social media
- Customer service
- Promoted listings
- Market your Etsy store offline
- If sales are poor

- ✓ Get reviews and publicity
- ✓ Blogging
- ✓ Etsy apps
- ✓ Mailing list

Pre-Setup Steps

- ☐ Brand your Etsy shop by naming it with your business name. The name shows up in your Etsy shop URL Example: etsy.com/shop/YourBizName
- ☐ Decide what you will sell and make a list of your products. For ideas, review Chapter 1. Each product will have its own listing.
- ☐ Research popular keywords buyers use to find products like yours (EtsyRank.com).
- ☐ Write a description for each product.
- ☐ Take photos of your items from different angles. Etsy allows you ten images for each product.
- ☐ Read and follow all the guidelines and store policies when setting up your shop.

Setting Up Your Etsy Shop

- ☐ Set up your payment methods so Etsy can send money direct to your bank when sales go through.
- ☐ Add your product listings with title, description, tags, category, size, colors, price, quantity, materials, occasions, and other attributes.

Shop Info and Appearance

- ☐ Add your artist's story to your Seller's Bio. Shoppers want to know about your creative journey.
- ☐ Your "Shop Announcement" is a place to add interesting details about your products and your creative process. It is also an area for placing popular keyword phrases used by Etsy shoppers.

- [ ] Design and upload a shop icon, profile image of yourself and (optional) store banner.

Shop Policies

- [ ] Write a welcome message. If natural, weave in popular search terms. They won't help you here with Etsy search rankings, but will help you get found by Google.

- [ ] Create your Payment, Shipping, Refund, Seller, and Additional Information policies. Don't omit these, as Etsy search favors shops with completed policies.

Shipping

- [ ] You can set up shipping profiles that explain how and where you ship to.

Improve Your Product Listings

Product listings are pages that display information to viewers about your product. Listings include images, a title, a product description, tags, price, shipping, quantity, and materials.

- [ ] When setting up a product listing, fill in each section. Each of the areas on the listing page provides another opportunity to appear in searches.

- [ ] Create separate listings for each color of the same item. Each listing is an added entrance to your shop through search. For example, people search for red scarves, black scarves, brown scarves, and more colors. If you make a listing for a red scarf and a separate listing for a black scarf and another listing for a brown scarf, you have tripled your potential landing pages.

- [ ] If you have customer reviews, include them in your product listing description. Even though viewers can access your reviews elsewhere, repeating one or more of the best ones in the description adds social proof that your product is worth buying.

> 📢 **ECO-FRIENDLY ETSY SELLERS FEATURED ON BLOG**
>
> Popular Earth911 blog featured earth-friendly gift makers. The article reported on notebooks made from recycled paper and elephant dung (it's true), bird feeders constructed using recycled wood and plastic, and handmade sunglasses framed using wood from repurposed skateboards. Source: Earth911.com/how-and-buy/eco-friendly-gifts-for-women/

IMAGES

Images play a major role when online shoppers browse your listings. Take photos of an item from different angles. Include images of people using your item and images of the product with a plain white background. See Appendix 1 for more on photography.

ETSY SEO

In the previous chapter, you learned the basics of SEO. In Chapter 1, you saw keyword search terms used by buyers looking for recycled handmade products. Now it's time for SEO tips specifically aimed at helping your Etsy shop listings get found more often in searches.

- ☐ The most important areas for SEO of your Etsy listings are titles, tags, and descriptions.

- ☐ Popular search terms (gathered from EtsyRank or Marmalead) used in your listing titles, tags, and descriptions can also be worked into other areas of your store like your story, shop policies, and announcements.

- [ ] Etsy allows you thirteen keyword tags for each listing. Use all of them. As much as possible, your listing's title should match your tags.

- [ ] Include related search terms in your product listing description.

- [ ] Categories are search terms themselves. Don't waste tags by using the same keyword as both a category and a tag. For instance, if you create a listing under the category of "tote bags," do not use one of your thirteen allowable tags for "tote bags."

- [ ] Use Etsy's "Search analytics." Access it through Shop Manager > Marketing > Search analytics. It's not so useful for new sellers because there isn't much traffic or sales to analyze. But if you have been on Etsy awhile and made sales, the search analytics tool will tell you which search words shoppers used to find your items converted to sales. Search analytics revealed my shop was getting traffic for search terms I had not used in my tags or listing titles. I went back in and added the terms as tags in a few listings and sales increased.

Product Descriptions

- [ ] In your product descriptions, tell the customer how your item will transform their life. Features are great, but benefits scll. If applicable, how many ways can a person use your item?

- [ ] Spell-check your listings before posting. When shoppers see misspelled words or grammatical errors, they may imagine your item is as carelessly assembled as your text.

- [ ] Add a shipping profile or select a shipping profile you want to update. Fill out the shipping profile. Select your order processing time (how long will it take to ship your order.) The shorter the processing time, the more you will convert visitors to customers.

☐ Price your items to make a profit. See Chapter 5 for how to do it.

Share on Social Media

After you have posted your listings, it's time to share. Etsy makes it easy for you to share your product listings, five-star reviews, items that have been recently favorited, and special sales to your social profiles on Pinterest, Facebook, Instagram, and Twitter. We'll go more in depth on these social media sites in later chapters.

To make use of this feature, go to your Shop Manager > Marketing > Social Media and then look for the tab near the top that reads "Social accounts." From there, connect your other social profiles. After you have connected your social profiles to Etsy, you are ready to post. Look for and click on the "+Create Post" button. Then Etsy walks you through creating and sharing a post to all your sites. Etsy's tool is free.

If posting frequently is taking too much of your time, schedule your social sharing with tools (subscriptions) like Buffer.com, Hootsuite.com or Tailwindapp.com.

📣 **ETSY SELLERS RECYCLE MEN'S TIES**

```
Many men have loads of ties they tire of
wearing. Smart crafters are repurposing and
selling those ties as wallets, dresses, quilts,
purses, baskets, and more. Source: WSJ.com/
articles/knotty-problem-what-to-do-with-a-
closet-full-of-old-ties-11575304256
```

Customer Service

☐ Be available. It builds goodwill. When I get a message from an Etsy shopper with a question, I respond right away. Customers always thank me for my prompt reply.

☐ Etsy allows you to program a *Thank-You* message that goes out automatically upon a sale. Express your gratitude for their purchase and tell them when they can expect to get their order.

☐ Another way to automate building customer relationships is to create a discount coupon for the next purchase. You have the option to set it to go to every customer upon checkout. Go to Shop Manager > Marketing > Sales and Coupons.

☐ If you get complaints, offer to replace the problem item or issue a refund. Put the customer in control. Don't make them feel they are wrong.

☐ Just fix problems, even if doing so costs you extra. You've heard the saying "the customer is always right." It has never been more true than with online sales.

☐ If you receive a negative review, get in touch with the customer and take care of any issues. After you have made things right, ask the disgruntled shopper to alter their negative rating. Offer a refund or substantial discount coupon, if it means getting better feedback.

☐ Print and include a packing slip that Etsy creates for each order so customers know where the product is coming from. I write on it a big "Thank-You" with the person's name at the top.

☐ Let shoppers know when they can expect their order to ship and make it as soon as you confidently can. Click Shop Manager > Settings > Shipping settings.

Promoted Listings

A way to potentially boost your Etsy sales is through their "Etsy Ads" feature under "Marketing" in your "Shop Manager."

Choose listings you want to promote and set a daily spending budget. Set your initial budget at the minimum so you can affordably test results. After a few weeks, go back in and view your promoted listings statistics.

If you haven't read Chapter 5 on pricing and calculated your profit margins, do it **before testing any ads**. You will need to know your margins before you can look at your stats to determine if you made or lost money through Etsy ads.

Etsy does the keyword analysis for the ads—you don't have to do anything except turn the "Etsy Ads" feature on and set a budget. You only pay when someone clicks through from an ad to your product listing.

Market Your Etsy Store Offline

Funneling offline shoppers to your Etsy store helps you gather more reviews and build social proof.

Wear or carry something you make whenever you leave the house. When someone comments, hand them your business card—printed with your Etsy store URL—and enthusiastically tell them, "you can see my entire line at my Etsy store!"

Over twenty percent of my Etsy buyers come from my business cards collected by shoppers visiting my craft show booths.

Home parties and trunk shows are other venues for mentioning your Etsy store.

If Sales Are Poor

- [ ] If your Etsy shop has been up for a while but performing poorly, hire successful Etsy sellers to critique it. You can get shop reviews on Etsy for anywhere from $20 to $100 or more. Save money at Fiverr.com and search for "etsy review."

- [ ] When using Fiverr, only work with providers who have all five-star reviews. I bought three reviews because I wanted different perspectives of my shop. You might think all of them would offer the same suggestions. Though on some points they agreed, each of the reviewers gave unique ideas that helped my sales.

- [ ] Browse the community forums and teams (groups) on Etsy to learn and share experiences with other craft artists about setting up, marketing, and running an Etsy store.

- [ ] List more items. Increasing the number of your product listings can boost your sales. You'll have more pages through which shoppers can find you. And Etsy search appears to favor shops that have more items than other sellers in the same category.

- [ ] Run discount coupons for key shopping dates. Etsy provides you with a calendar of peak buying seasons with tips for tying in special offers. Go to Shop Manager > Marketing > Key shopping dates.

- [ ] Boost sales by offering free shipping, if your profit margin allows it. Etsy created a seller option called *Guaranteed Free Shipping* for orders over $35. Sellers who opt in to the program get priority in search results over sellers who do not offer free shipping. You can also go into your Shop Manager > Marketing > Sales and coupons. By using Etsy's free shipping coupon (choose "no end date"), Etsy displays a free shipping badge on your shop's product pages. If you set up free shipping as a shipping option, you won't get the Etsy badge. The Etsy badge helps your listings show up better in search results. Even if you have to raise your prices to cover shipping, it will increase your visits and sales.

📢 **ETSY TRENDS SEE GROWTH IN ECO-FRIENDLY**

```
Dayna Isom Johnson, Etsy's trend expert says
more and more people want to use recycled
materials or natural dyes. Etsy has seen a
forty-three percent year-over-year rise in all
categories for eco-friendly items. Source:
MarthaStewart.com
```

Get Reviews and Publicity

Shopping blogs actively seek new products to review. But the competition for these reviews can be tough. Magazines, newspapers, and freelance writers also report on earth-friendly and sustainable products they think will interest their readers.

Etsy Apps

Apps can help you market your Etsy shop. You can quickly link your social media profiles to your Etsy store through the integrations page at: etsy.com/your/shops/me/integrations

There are optional third-party apps built for users who have little technical background. Tools like Tailwindapp.com and HootSuite.com help you schedule and promote your Etsy product listings with social media.

Another tool is the *Etsy Seller App* for smartphones. With the *Shop Update* function, I can upload an image at an art or crafts fair, tag it to one of my product listings, and hit update. This update is then viewable by my previous customers and followers.

New apps for Etsy sellers are always being developed. Search for "Etsy seller apps _____" (fill in the current year) to get the most current Etsy seller tools available.

Mailing List

Etsy success relies heavily on repeat business. To get customers coming back, you need their permission to stay in touch. A mail list is the easiest, least-costly way for you to reach out to customers. Customer lists are so important, see Chapter 21 for how to get yours started and how to engage with your list to create loyal customers.

Etsy is great for learning how to set up and promote an e-commerce site for your handmade upcycled crafts. After you master Etsy selling, test other platforms or start your own website. The next chapter introduces more ways to sell online, including Handmade on Amazon.

CHAPTER 11

E-Commerce Alternatives to Etsy

Though Etsy may be the most popular market for handmade products, there are other options to help you grow your sales and broaden your online presence.

The Amazon Handmade category is available to Amazon's over 300 million shoppers. Sites like Artfire, Zibbet, and others also compete with Etsy to attract shoppers looking to buy handmade. Another option is setting up your own domain-name website.

With so many possibilities, you may feel you have to choose between them. But there is no rule that says you can only sell in one marketplace. Test them and measure the results. Then focus on any and all platforms that bring you sales and healthy profit margins.

In this chapter, you will learn about:
- Selling on Amazon Handmade
- Alternatives to Etsy and Amazon
- Getting a domain-name website
- Blogging

SELLING ON AMAZON HANDMADE

Amazon Handmade opened in 2015. Reviews by maker-sellers have been mixed. Those who have done well report better sales than Etsy. My own Amazon Handmade sales are twice that of my Etsy sales, though my profit margin is much lower per sale.

Applying and getting set up as a seller on Amazon Handmade is more complex than other online marketplaces for handmade products. The application link is: https://services.amazon.com/handmade/handmade.html

If accepted, you must subscribe to their Professional Account for sellers. The monthly charge of around $40 was being waived for Handmade sellers as an incentive, but that could change by the time you read this book.

On the plus side, Amazon has a huge marketplace of buyers. Sellers get access to Seller Central, a back office with in-depth analytics and reports on how often your item was viewed, clicked on, and sold.

What to know about selling on Amazon Handmade:

- [ ] Seller fees are fifteen percent of the retail price. This is higher than Etsy's five percent. Calculate your profit margins before you sign up. (Check sites for current fee structure.)

- [ ] Setting up product page listings is straightforward. You can copy and paste your Etsy listings content.

- [ ] Your products may sell great on Amazon, but do poorly on Etsy and vice versa. Test product listings on both sites over a month's time to learn what sells where.

- [ ] Amazon Handmade gives you an Artisan's Profile, where you can paste in your artist story and upload images of yourself.

- [ ] Amazon allows sellers to promote their handmade products through Sponsored Product ads. You can access reports that reveal which keyword searches result in sales. You can also learn how the cost of your ads compares to your sales. This lets you adjust your ads to run only those that result in a healthy profit margin.

- [ ] If your profit margin allows, consider FBA (Fulfilled By Amazon). Through this program, you ship (at your expense) your products to Amazon warehouses. They fulfill orders to their more than ninety million Amazon Prime member buyers. Amazon Prime members get free shipping and buy more often than non-members.

- [ ] An alternative way to tap into Amazon Prime buyers is to use Seller-Fulfilled Prime. Under this program, your buyers get free shipping (because you agree to pay it) but you do the packing and shipping instead of sending products to Amazon FBA warehouses.

- [ ] With 85% of Amazon shoppers reporting they hesitate to make a purchase because of shipping charges, offering free shipping sets you apart from most sellers.

- [ ] If you don't use FBA or Seller Fulfilled Prime, you must set up shipping settings.

- [ ] As with all e-commerce sites, SEO plays a big role in getting views and sales from a site's marketplace. Go to the Amazon Handmade category and start typing in words that describe your product. Amazon will start to auto-populate your search with suggested keywords. Those suggested words come from searches that have resulted in sales.

- [ ] Place the most popular keywords at the beginning of your title and your product descriptions. Amazon allows for additional keywords—similar to Etsy tags—in each listing.

- [ ] You can also use a service like MerchantWords.com to discover buyer search terms. Starting from your own list of words and phrases, MerchantWords delivers a list of keywords you may not have thought of. You'll also see how strong the competition is for your products.

- [ ] Make customer service your top priority. Amazon shoppers weigh other buyer reviews before making purchases. Double-check your product and packaging quality before shipping. Be willing to refund an unhappy customer.

- [ ] Amazon has a forum where you can ask and answer questions to other sellers called Amazon's Handmade Community. You will find answers and be able to ask questions of other sellers.

SELL ARTS & CRAFTS FROM UPCYCLED MATERIALS

> 🔊 **REPURPOSING TEXTILES**
>
> ```
> Emma Balder works with repurposed textiles
> and recycled thread. She collects scraps from
> other artists as well as fashion designers
> and upholsterers. Some of her work has taken
> form as large public art installations. She's
> also created pieces for Meow Wolf and PepsiCo.
> Source: The Houston Chronicle.
> ```

ALTERNATIVES TO ETSY AND AMAZON

Though Etsy and Amazon Handmade have the largest buyer marketplaces for handmade products, there are other sites worth checking out. The top Etsy and Amazon Handmade alternatives in the US:

BigCartel.com
Zibbet.com
IndieMade.com
iCraftGifts.com
eCrater.com
Bonanza.com

See Appendix 3 for more places to sell online around the world.

Some seller sites charge a small percentage when a sale is made. Some charge a monthly or yearly fee and allow you to upload as many listings as you want. Each site has a different set of terms, so read the fine print to avoid surprises.

SETTING UP YOUR OWN DOMAIN SITE

Many sellers prefer having a domain-name website. With your own site, you are independent of whatever changes a large outfit like Etsy or Amazon makes.

One of the big complaints about Etsy, Amazon, and the other online shop providers is that they *own* the customers, not you. Setting up your own domain site lets you blog, capture e-mails, provide a customer newsletter, offer specials, announce new products, and otherwise operate like other e-commerce sites.

Building a site from scratch can be stressful and time-consuming. Using services and tools like Wix or Wordpress allows you to set up a basic site in less than an hour.

- [ ] Your business name is the best choice for your domain name, as it helps you brand your business. If you can't get the exact name, try adding a short word before or after your domain name and check for availability again.

- [ ] Once you settle on your name, register it at a site like NameCheap.com or GoDaddy.com. The annual fee to keep your domain name is anywhere from $9 to $20, depending on the registrar.

- [ ] After you have registered your domain name, you need a web host. Some registrars also provide hosting. If not, there are thousands to choose from. HostGator.com and BlueHost.com have received good reviews.

- [ ] All web hosts walk you through connecting your domain name to their servers so that your website will be visible online.

- [ ] The next step is creating and uploading pages with content. Sellers usually include: home page, about the artist page, shopping page, contact page, subscribe page, and a blog page if you plan to blog.

- [ ] Wordpress, a free web-building application available from most web hosts provides everything you need. Wordpress offers free themes, free e-commerce plugins and lots of free support. Wordpress sites are popular for e-commerce and for blogging.

- [ ] If you aren't using Wordpress with a shopping-cart plugin, you will need to build an online catalog and process transactions. Shopify and BigCommerce are two of the most popular shopping-cart programs.

> 📢 **PURCHASES OF "SUSTAINABLE" INCREASING**
>
> In a study sponsored by NYU (New York University) and IRI (Information Resources Inc) shopper purchasing from 2013 to 2018 was measured in thirty-six categories. Findings revealed a 50.1% growth in sales of "sustainable" products. "Sustainable" products grew 5.6 times faster than conventional products. Source: bit.ly/sustainablestudy

ONLINE ADVERTISING

Ad campaigns or promoted listings have paid off for some sellers, but not all. You can only know if they work for your products by testing. Limit your risk by setting a low daily budget for ad spending and an end date for a campaign.

As I mention several times, know your profit margins if you intend to grow your side hustle. Ads are one way to boost your sales, but there's no guarantee they will.

Before you start a campaign, determine how much you can afford and are willing to lose and then test ads. If your test ad campaign loses money, stop running the ads. If your test makes enough money that you still earn a profit from each sale, increase your ad spend / daily budget gradually, continuing to measure results.

Checklist for Running Ads

- ✓ Test ad campaigns with a small daily budget.
- ✓ Run ads long enough to get 2,000 impressions.
- ✓ Measure click-throughs and cost-of-sales.
- ✓ If you have the budget, test different audiences.
- ✓ Drop ads that don't result in sales.
- ✓ Gradually increase ad campaigns that convert at low cost-of-sales, continuing to monitor spending vs profit.

Where to Test Ad Campaigns:

- Etsy.com Find "Etsy Ads" feature under "Marketing" in "Shop Manager"

- Advertising.amazon.com
- Ads.pinterest.com
- Business.instagram.com/advertising/
- Ads.twitter.com
- Adwords.google.com
- Artdeadline.com – For makers of upcycled art, Artdeadline offers a variety of promotional services to paid subscribers. Their client base includes fine art galleries, art associations, art agencies and institutions, artist representatives, and others.
- Ads on shopping blog sites – Many of the larger blog sites accept ads. Look at the site's menu bar for a link to "Advertising."

Shopify

Shopify is a popular app that lets you sell your products online through many marketplaces. It allows you to customize a shopping cart from pre-designed themes with no need for skills or previous experience in building a website.

Shopify integrates with Amazon, Etsy, eBay, Google, Instagram, Facebook, Pinterest, Lyst, your own website and many other platforms.

Shopify is a monthly subscription service, starting at a basic level for $29 a month.

📢 **FROM TRASH TO ART**

The average American generates about four pounds of trash per day. Rather than throw it away, create works of art. Federico Uribe, from Columbia, crafts art collages by repurposing old pencils, used keys, fabric, wire and other materials destined for junkyards. Source: Magazine.art21.org

---

Just ahead, another way to market online is by publishing interesting content through blogging, which is mostly free except for the time you invest. For some sellers, blogging has paid off with increased sales and a larger mailing list of followers.

CHAPTER 12

Blogging

Adding a blog to your marketing mix allows you to publish articles, images and videos around topics related to your handmade products and grow your e-mail mailing list. Search engines love new content so blog pages can rank higher in Google search results than static web pages.

Blogging is a way to express yourself without editing, an instant way to get published, a journal from which to sprout product news, and a way to create community.

It's also a way to attract and stay in touch with new customers. People who read your blog get to know you as a human being rather than a marketer.

Each blog post is an article page. The more pages you have on your site, the more opportunities to get found in Google search results.

You can create free blogs on Wordpress.org, Blogger.com, Medium.com and many other places. Or you can buy a domain name, get it hosted and publish a blog from the site using Wordpress as a platform.

Wordpress is the most popular and the easiest blogging platform. Go on YouTube and search for "wordpress tutorial" to find hundreds of free videos that walk you through the process step-by-step.

Statistics show blogging is effective for sellers because:

- 81% of U.S. online consumers rely on advice from blogs. (Blogher.com)

- 61% of U.S. online consumers have bought something based on reviews from a blog. (Blogher.com)

- Small businesses that blog get 125% more lead growth than those that don't. (ThinkCreative)

- 92% of businesses that blog more than once per day have acquired a customer from their blog. (Hubspot.com.)

Tips for blogging success:

☐ Articles with images and videos of your handmade products get almost 100% more views, so make your posts media-rich.

☐ Post useful content like how-to-upcycle articles, statistics about how much trash goes into landfills, related products to yours, consumer-environmental trends, news, and resources.

☐ For every seven to ten useful content posts, write a post that pitches one of your products like a new product, sale, or event where you'll be displaying.

☐ Wordpress plugins, Zapier.com and IFTTT.com let you automatically syndicate posts and images from your blogs to multiple social media sites.

☐ Wordpress plugins like *Etsy Shop* (free) let you connect and display your Etsy shop listings so you don't have to use a separate shopping cart to process transactions.

☐ Use EtsyRank.com to research popular search words and phrases that Etsy shoppers use every day to find products like yours. Place those words and phrases in your blog article's title, URL, content, image file names, and tags.

Link to your blog posts on social media. But promoting through social media takes finesse and time. The next few chapters explore the tools and best practices that save you time while attracting more visitors to your blog, website, and your product listings on Etsy and elsewhere.

CHAPTER 13

Introduction to Social Media

Social media sites offer multiple ways to grow a fan base for your handmade products. Followers on each site engage distinctively. For instance, Facebook fans follow behaviour patterns that differ from Instagramers who differ from Tik-Tok users or Pinterest followers.

Converting followers to customers requires learning each social site's culture. Aim at getting results on only one or two of your favorite social sites you are at ease with before taking on others.

To help you master social media marketing, this chapter covers:
- Advantages of social media
- Social marketing tips
- Social posts scheduling tools
- Get followers on your e-mail list

ADVANTAGES OF SOCIAL MEDIA

Handmade sellers spend time on social networking sites to gather new leads, increase sales, and follow up with customers. They find they can:
- Post product images and videos easily and quickly
- Learn how customers think, message, and act
- Engage with customers in more friendly ways
- Grow a following
- Send more visitors to an Etsy shop or website
- Discover what sellers with similar products are doing to market their things
- Test ads across different social platforms

> 📣 **INSPIRING YOUTH VIA RECYCLED ART**
>
> Wichita Falls, Texas hosts an annual Home & Garden Festival with a Youth Recycled Arts Contest that encourages kindergarten to 12th-grade students to create artistic pieces made from recyclable materials. Submissions can be painting, sculpture, or other visual artworks. Over $1,500 given in awards for winners.

SOCIAL MARKETING TIPS

Before we go into the four main social platforms, the following checklist acts as a primer for successful social posting:

- ☐ Get familiar with each platform. People hang out on social sites for specific reasons. Something that gets your Instagram posts noticed may not work on Pinterest or Twitter.
- ☐ Start with a social site you feel most at ease with.
- ☐ Have realistic expectations. Reports show that only 1% to 2% of social site referrals buy on their first visit to a site.
- ☐ Some sellers say Instagram sends them more customers. For others, it's Pinterest or Facebook. Which is best for you? Test your product line and measure your results.
- ☐ Brief social media posts with fewer than seventy characters get better engagement than longer posts.
- ☐ Post more than once a day. Use tools described later in this chapter to schedule post deliverance across several sites. These tools also give you analytics to measure your post's engagement.

- [ ] Posts with images get more shares on Facebook and the most retweets on Twitter.
- [ ] Posts with videos get the most engagement.
- [ ] The organic reach of your posts is limited. To get more viewers, you will have to pay up in the form of ads or post boosts.
- [ ] When people comment on your posts, reply. The more interaction you can inspire, the more your posts will show up organically.
- [ ] For every seven posts that help, entertain or educate, post a product-related article or link. Repeat the cycle a few times and notice what your followers do. A more conservative option is to post one promo for every ten "giving" posts.

📢 **TRASHION ARTIST INVITED TO U.N. EXHIBIT**

The UN's SEA of Solutions showcases wearable art made entirely from used plastic bottles. The goal is to bring together world leaders, businesses, scientists, and community organizations to help stop ocean plastic pollution. Francis Sollano from Cebu is the only Filipino artist invited to exhibit his recycled artworks at the SEA of Solutions. He makes "trashion" or wearable art from trash. Sollano also creates products for the home by upcycling junk.

Francis is also executive director of Youth for a Livable Cebu, where he focuses on environmental and civic causes. His campaigns on climate change and urban sustainability has become an inspiration for other communities to conduct their own programs. For more about his work, see FranciSollano.com. Source: CebuDailyNews.Inquirer.net

Social Posts Scheduling Tools

Managing many profiles individually can quickly take up your day. In Chapter 10, Selling on Etsy, one of the tools in your Etsy Shop Manager under Marketing is the Social Media option. You can quickly connect and promote posts of your listings, reviews and favorites directly to your Facebook, Instagram, Pinterest, and Twitter profiles.

Scheduling tools make posting to multiple platforms even easier. You could create a bunch of posts ahead of time and then schedule them to go out on given days.

Scheduling tools help leverage your time by promoting your products to all of your social media accounts through one interface. The tools below cost a small monthly subscription. I suggest you try them for a month (some offer free trials), measure your results, and then decide if you want to stay with that tool or try a different one.

- Outfy.com
- Hootsuite.com
- Buffer.com
- Tailwindapp.com
- SproutSocial.com

Get Followers on Your Mailing List

You don't own your social followers, but you do own your mailing list. And that list will be yours to promote through regardless of what happens to your social platforms.

If your favorite social site folds, changes policies, or if your account gets shut down, all of your followers and the work you did to get them vanishes. There is no back-up.

To get your followers to give you their e-mail addresses, you may need to offer an incentive like a coupon, free download, a newsletter subscription, or a mini-course.

Your e-mail list is an asset. Back it up frequently. Use it to stay in touch with your tribe. See Chapter 21 for tips on capturing and making use of your mailing list.

The next chapters go deeper into how to make the most of your resources when marketing on the four major social media sites, starting with Facebook.

CHAPTER 14

Facebook Best Practices

Over two billion people use Facebook. They spend an average of thirty-five minutes each day on the site and almost eighty percent of shoppers in the US have found products to buy while on Facebook.

Once you have a personal profile set up on Facebook, you can set up a free Facebook Page for your business. Facebook personal profiles are limited to 5,000 friends you can add. But Facebook Pages can have an unlimited number of likes and followers.

Your Facebook Page

- [ ] FB pages let you add content about your products and sell them from the page. You also have access to "Insights" providing visitor data you can't get from a profile page like how many people your posts reached, how many new likes you got, how many people engaged with your posts, and more.

- [ ] Sell directly from your Facebook Page by enabling a Facebook Shop tab in your page settings. Shoppers can browse your items, make a purchase, and pay for it while remaining on your Facebook Page.

- [ ] Alternatively, the Shop tab can link to your other website or your Etsy shop. But sending customers away from Facebook creates an added step they have to take and will lower conversion rates.

- [ ] To collect payments, set up an account with a payment gateway like Stripe.com. After your payment account is open, add products in your store. For a detailed video on setting up a Facebook Shop, see http://bit.ly/setupfacebookstore

Posting on Facebook

- [ ] As mentioned in the chapter on Selling On Etsy, you can post to Facebook directly from your Etsy Shop Manager > Marketing > Social media.

- [ ] Or use an app that integrates your Etsy or other online store products directly with your Facebook Shop. Shopify, BigCommerce, and other e-commerce platforms will link your item listings on their platform to display on your Facebook Page.

- [ ] Getting sales from Facebook means getting visual, big-time. Studies show Facebook users respond more to imagery and video than simple text.

- [ ] Post several times a week—at least once a week—consistently from your FB Page, not your personal profile.

- [ ] Upload photos of your products, videos of your creative process and attention-getting posts with a mix of video, imagery, and text.

- [ ] Post how-to tips on recycling, repurposing, and reusing.

- [ ] Video content rules on Facebook. People stay tuned five times longer to videos than they do posts without video. Thirty percent of mobile FB users report that video is their favorite way to find new products.

- [ ] Facebook Live videos get six times the interactions as regular videos. FB Live videos rank higher in newsfeeds.

- [ ] Post useful tips related to your products. If you make accessories, offer tips like "5 *ways to use this* ____ *to look great in a hurry while helping the planet.*"

- [ ] Humor is good, but take care not to use jokes that could offend someone.

- [ ] When describing your own products, elaborate on how you are helping save the planet in your posts. Use Google to find and cite statistics about landfill waste and how supporting businesses like yours reduces the landfill burden.

Facebook Stories

- [ ] As a person's feed fills up with incoming posts, your message quickly gets lost as newer stories push it down. FB Stories appear above your users' feed and remain there for 24 hours. If you add to your Story several times a day, it keeps your business name in front of your fans instead of it vanishing in the feed.

- [ ] Add Stories to your FB page from your smartphone. They can be made up of photos, videos, and text content.

- [ ] Stories work best when they convey a "behind the scenes" look into your recycling business. For example, you might shoot a video of you creating a new piece. Or, for fun, completely messing one up. Think of it as reality TV about your business.

"Buy Sell" Groups on Facebook

- [ ] FB "Buy Sell" groups for handmade products allow you to post images, product descriptions, and (usually) links directly to your item's sales page. For example, see Facebook.com/groups/craftsu.

- [ ] To find other groups on FB, type "buy sell handmade" or "buy sell crafts" in the search bar at the upper left of any FB page. Then click on the Groups tab to narrow results to only look at Groups. Be sure to read the rules of any group you join before posting.

- [ ] At first, you might think the members of these groups are all sellers. However, they do attract buyers who use search terms like "seeking _____" or "anyone make_____?"

Facebook Marketplace

- [ ] Facebook.com/marketplace/ is FB's own buy/sell market. It's used by 800 million people globally each month. Sellers list items for sale. Shoppers browse for bargains. Like with Craigslist, there is no fee to use the marketplace.

- [ ] The FB Marketplace displays tons of stuff people are looking to get rid of at low prices. Search results are tailored to your local area.

- [ ] A search for "handmade" brought up hundreds of items near me. Most of the listings were pre-owned items. Some were new and priced at the same retail price the seller asks on Etsy.

- [ ] Though listing handmade products next to used stuff won't set your products apart, your item on FB Marketplace gives you a virtual shopping cart for free. You can link directly to your product listing, buyers can pay through Facebook Payments, and you can ship the item or deliver it locally. A big plus: the buyer never has to leave Facebook to complete the transaction.

Facebook Ads and Boost Posts

For promoting posts to more viewers, you can boost posts or run Facebook Ads. Ads can link directly to a product in your Facebook Store. Start out with a small daily ad spend budget. Measure your ad results. Tweak and test again. Repeat and expand your budget for ads that pull in sales. Discontinue ads that aren't profitable.

📢 **THE IMPACT OF RECYCLING PAPER**

Seventeen trees could be spared for every 2,000 pounds of paper recycled, along with saving 4,000 kilowatts of energy, over 300 gallons of oil, and 7,000 gallons of water. Source: University of Southern Indiana

CHAPTER 15

Pinterest Best Practices

Pinterest.com is a visual search engine where you pin your favorite images and videos from across the web. Pins on Pinterest don't expire, so investing time here can pay off in the long term.

The site gets over two billion searches each month. It's considered by many to be the most popular visual search platform. More relevant to sellers, 93% percent of pinners use Pinterest for planning purchases. For example, fans of Pinterest use it to plan weddings, baby arrivals, style tips, special events, find recipes, DIY how-tos, and much more.

The average sale arising from a Pinterest search is close to $60–higher than average sales from Twitter or Facebook buyers.

Setting Up Your Profile

- [ ] Choose the Pinterest business account option when registering. It offers more options including access to Pinterest Analytics, which tracks and measures how engaging your pins are.

- [ ] If you already have a personal profile, convert it to a business account for free.

- [ ] When setting up your profile, use the same business name across all of your online sites.

- [ ] As with every place you sell online, include popular tags/keywords related to your business in your profile description and when naming your boards so you get discovered in searches.

- [ ] Add a link to your website or Etsy store.

- [ ] Fill in all the areas in your profile to get the most

from Pinterest's site traffic. Include popular search terms so your profile has a better chance of showing up in searches.

- [ ] Go to "Settings" and "Claim." Add your website if you have one. Also, claim your Etsy store, Instagram, and YouTube accounts. Claiming your accounts gives you access to Analytics that show how visitors engage with your pins.

Creating Boards

- [ ] Pinterest boards let you organize your images by topics. After you have set up your profile, your next step is to create five to ten boards to place your pins in.

- [ ] Collect a mix of content that people will enjoy looking through. For example, if you knit or crochet scarves from sustainable materials, create one board for pins of your scarves, another board with pins teaching people different ways to wear scarves, another board with interesting recycling tips, and another board that shows your scarves worn on special occasions.

- [ ] If you don't have a lot of product images of your own to fill in your boards in the beginning, fill your boards with images of related tips, guides, and products you like.

- [ ] Choose a popular keyword tag for the board name. Include a description using several related keywords. Upload an eye-catching cover image. Just as people judge a book by its cover, they explore your pins based on your boards' cover images.

- [ ] For examples of how to build out your boards, just search Pinterest using words that describe your products or customers, make a list of the most popular pinners, and observe how they've created their boards and pins.

Gathering Followers

- [ ] Search for topics related to your products and find the most popular boards. When you find someone with a million or more followers, click the "Followers" link on their profile. A drop-down list appears. Start following the popular pinners' followers that appear to be active on Pinterest.

- [ ] Follow up to fifty new people every day. If you have set up your boards with interesting image collections, you will quickly find the popular pinners' followers following you. This is one of the fastest ways to build your own following. To keep the growth happening, pin new images daily as they show up in your new follower's feeds.

- [ ] Join group boards that allow you to pin your handmade products to their boards. Google "Pinterest group boards for Etsy sellers." You will discover loads of promotional opportunities like those at: http://thesavvyetsymarketer.com/31-etsy-group-boards-pinterest-join.

- [ ] Engage with your followers. Comment on their pins. Create conversations.

Pinning

- [ ] Most Pinterest users are female, so think of pins that will appeal to women.

- [ ] Pin consistently; even daily.

- [ ] Pin images and videos viewers can't resist saving or repinning. Pin helpful tips.

- [ ] Pin your product images.

- [ ] Pinterest favors pins/pinners that get higher engagement (saves, repins, click-throughs) with higher search results.

- [ ] Pictures tell stories. Studies reveal that lifestyle images get more attention than product images; 150% more purchases than product photos alone.

PINTEREST BEST PRACTICES

- [ ] Videos pinned on Pinterest get higher engagement than other sites.

- [ ] Optimize each pin to get more viewers from search. Each pin can have a description. In the description use popular search terms and tags related to your products. Link directly to your product's listing on Etsy or elsewhere so viewers can click to buy instantly.

- [ ] Prior to holidays, searches on Pinterest reflect heightened interest in Valentine's Day, Mother's Day, and so on. Pin with tags and keywords relative to holidays to take advantage of special occasions.

- [ ] As mentioned earlier, you can pin your Etsy listings, five-star reviews, and more on Pinterest through your Etsy Shop Manager.

- [ ] Not everyone who views your pins or follows you on Pinterest will click through to your online store, but enough do to justify investing time here. Even when I have neglected pinning for long periods, my Etsy store statistics show visitors checking out my items from Pinterest almost every day.

- [ ] Rich pins are a special format that gives more context around an idea or product by displaying extra information on the pin. Rich pins are free, but your pins have to meet requirements and be approved. The steps for setting up rich pins are at: help.pinterest.com/en/business/article/rich-pins

- [ ] With a business account on Pinterest, you can advertise through Promoted Pins. As with all ad campaigns, set your spending budget at the minimum dollar amounts, and test for two to three weeks. Pinterest provides ad tracking that reveals how many people view your ads and click through.

CHAPTER 16

Instagram Best Practices

Instagram is a photo-sharing app that lets you post images from your smartphone to your Instagram account. It is a mobile-dominated platform for telling visual stories—98% of content comes from phones.

While Instagram has over a billion users, 59% are under thirty years old. Many Etsy sellers report they get more sales via Instagram than Pinterest or Facebook. Understandable, since over 1,926,000 Instagram users follow Etsy's profile there.

Instagram members have a high engagement rate. Over 70% of users have bought something found there using their mobile phone.

Set Up an Instagram Account

- [ ] Download the Instagram app and install on your phone. If you plan to use Instagram to promote your handmade upcycled items, set up your new account as a business account. Or convert your existing profile to a business one.

- [ ] Like with other social sites, a business account allows you to promote or advertise your posts. You also get access to "Insights" (analytics) about your posts, hashtags, visitors, and engagements.

- [ ] Choose the same username (or a close variant if taken) that you use on Etsy and all your social media profiles. Upload the same profile image you use on other social sites.

- [ ] Include a link to your Etsy or other online shop in your profile.

Posting Images

- [ ] With the app open, take a photo with your phone, write a cute caption, and push "share." You have the option to add image-editing filters before you share your photos.

- [ ] The app automatically sizes your uploaded image to display on mobile devices. Horizontal (portrait) oriented images fit the screen well as most people naturally hold their phones horizontally.

- [ ] Sharing images comes with options. You can share to your other social media profiles. You can add hashtags. You can tag other people in the image. And you can add your geo-location so viewers will know where the image was taken.

- [ ] You can also upload images from your computer.

- [ ] Add a brief caption to your post. Caption text is found through search, so include relevant hashtags.

Videos

- [ ] Instagram lets you add and edit videos up to sixty seconds long. Videos can come directly from your phone or from content you have transferred to your phone from another source.

- [ ] Shared videos tell interesting stories.

- [ ] Sellers can add a call-to-action at the end of a video. Just add a line of text in the final moments. That text may be your only chance to get your message out. Instagram videos display in silence until viewers tap the phone to turn on sound.

Instagram Stories

- [ ] Instagram Stories, like FB Stories, feature your photos and videos at the top of your follower's feeds. They remain there for twenty-four hours.

- [ ] Upload your story-behind-the-scenes of your handmade recycling side hustle. Post stories about

SELL ARTS & CRAFTS FROM UPCYCLED MATERIALS

how you got started in your side hustle, how you make your products, and what inspires you.

☐ Use the "poll" feature to ask your followers questions. Discover what they think about your stories.

📢 **RECYCLED PUPPET PARADE INSPIRES CHANGE**

Athens, Ohio is home to Honey for the Heart, sponsor of an art exhibit and parade that showcases its costume-sized, recycled artistic puppets. The art puppets are crafted from repurposed junk with a vision to inspire people to realize they have the power to recreate our environment. Source: ThePostAthens.com

---

Hashtags

☐ Hashtags are mashed-up phrases preceded by the # sign. Example: #handmadewedding. The # sign turns the phrase into a clickable link. Hashtags help your posts get found in search.

☐ Hashtags can help you uncover other sellers with products like yours.

☐ Multi-worded hashtags help you attract buyers instead of just researchers. If you make and sell repurposed wedding items, broad topic hashtags like #weddings won't be as useful to you as more specific hashtags like #recycledweddingstationary, or #ecofriendlyweddingsouvenir.

☐ Use relevant keywords. Avoid including hashtags just because the words are popular search terms.

☐ Use apps to find hashtags related to your niche like keywordtool.io, displaypurposes.com, skedsocial.com, hashtagify.me or all-hashtag.com. AutoHash is a mobile app that analyzes your images and suggests hashtags.

INSTAGRAM BEST PRACTICES

- [ ] You can add up to thirty hashtags when you post or comment, but adding so many looks spammy. The fix is to add a comment and include hashtags in the comment.
- [ ] Studies show posts with multiple hashtags get twice the amount of interaction with viewers.
- [ ] Mix your choice of hashtags among your posts and comments.
- [ ] Reserve one hashtag to brand yourself. Hashtag your Instagram name.
- [ ] Look at the posts on the most popular profiles in your niche. See hashtags you had not thought of? Start adding relevant ones to your content.
- [ ] After your profile has gotten likes, comments, and followers over time use the "Insights" feature in your business account to discover which hashtags brought the most traffic to your Etsy store or website.
- [ ] Find keywords by starting to type in the search bar at Instagram and note the auto-complete drop-down list of popular tags. Instagram's auto-complete comes from actual searches.
- [ ] Save all your hashtags in a text file or spreadsheet. Separate them by niches, products, people, or other categories. When you need hashtags, just go to your file and copy them.
- [ ] Use hashtags for communities grown up around your product's niche.

Where to place hashtags?

- As a sticker on your images and videos
- Your post's description
- Comments you leave
- Comments you get
- Your Instagram Stories
- Your profile bio

Tips for posting

- [ ] Popularity rises from increased likes, comments, and shares. The more your images touch viewers, the more engagement you will get.
- [ ] When someone likes or comments on your image posts, send them a thank-you. It's a natural way to start a conversation.
- [ ] If your creative muse takes a vacation, post other people's content.
- [ ] Monitor your followers through Instagram's insights regularly to learn how people engage with your posts and hashtags.
- [ ] Study the posts of the most popular Instagram profiles in your niche. Look for content that attracted the most comments. This is a great way to get inspired for what you could post.
- [ ] Follow the followers of other sellers in your niche. If they appear to be frequent or recent posters, start liking their images. Many of them will follow you back.
- [ ] Follow Etsy sellers with complementary product lines to yours. Comment and like their content. Message them and see if they would like to cross-promote each other's lines.
- [ ] Post often. Uploading content twice a day has shown to increase followers. Too busy? Use one of the social media scheduling tools described earlier.
- [ ] Instagram is highly social. Tagging others (adding @personsusername) can earn goodwill and increase your post comments.

Instagram Advertising

- [ ] Like with most social platforms, you can promote your Instagram posts through paid advertising. For business accounts, the "Insights" function provides clues about which of your posts make good candidates for promoting.

☐ Start with a small budget and test. Target your ad to reach followers of popular sellers in your niche.

☐ As with all paid promotions, include a call-to-action. Make it clear what you want viewers to do: visit your Etsy shop, make a purchase, sign up for your newsletter, or other action.

☐ Monitor your Etsy shop stats closely when you run an Instagram or other ad campaign. Your Etsy stats will tell you if you are getting traffic from Instagram or other social network. If ads are working, increase your budget and try new audiences.

☐ If your ads do not result in profitable sales, stop the campaigns. Change your content, or your offer, or your audience.

📣 **THE IMPACT OF RECYCLING GLASS**

Recycling glass requires a lower temperature (less energy) than making new glass. Glass made from recycling lowers related air pollution by twenty percent and related water pollution by fifty percent. Making pretty things from glass keeps it out of landfills. Less glass lying around is safer for kids and everyone.

CHAPTER 17

TikTok Best Practices

Millions of people use TikTok every day. If you have consumed videos on the platform, you already have a reference for how to create your own content. For those new to the platform, see *How to Use TikTok* at https://blog.hootsuite.com/how-to-use-tiktok/.

SETTING UP BUSINESS ACCOUNT

- [ ] Set up a TikTok business account (or convert your personal account) to take advantage of extra features.
- [ ] In the TikTok app, tap Profile at the bottom.
- [ ] Tap the Menu button at the top.
- [ ] Tap Settings and privacy.
- [ ] Tap Manage account.
- [ ] Tap Switch to Business Account and follow the instructions provided to finish.
- [ ] As with your other social accounts, choose a username / handle or close version of your business name that helps identify your brand.

TIPS FOR YOUR VIDEOS

- [ ] Use a high quality camera/phone
- [ ] Make your videos short
- [ ] Be yourself, TikTok is all about real people doing interesting things
- [ ] Add sounds and visual effects to make your video pop
- [ ] Sample video ideas: a brief tour of your studio where you make your items, or a quick look at how you make stuff, or shoot how you pack an order to ship.
- [ ] TikTokkers follow trends and trends change frequently. Keep up with what's current at: https://fanbytes.co.uk/tiktok-trends-newsletter/

Growing Your Following

- [ ] Respond to comments. TikTok has the highest engagement of any social platform.list will be previous customers.
- [ ] Good videos rule, so make yours shine.
- [ ] Largest audience on TikTok is Gen Z (10 to 25 years old) so post when they are most active, 3pm to 9pm with Fridays and Saturdays being the best days.
- [ ] Start a challenge.
- [ ] Add trending sounds to your video. See: https://ads.tiktok.com/business/creativecenter/inspiration/popular/music/pc/en
- [ ] Avoid posting your videos from other sites on TikTok. TikTok's algorithm rewards original content with higher placements.
- [ ] For using TikTok to promote an Etsy shop: https://www.etsy.com/seller-handbook/article/1026011778660 Good tips here even if you are selling elsewhere online.
- [ ] Best TikTok accounts to follow if you sell on Etsy or elsewhere: https://goldcityventures.com/best-tiktok-accounts-for-etsy-sellers/

Hashtags

- [ ] Hashtags (putting the # sign before a keyword tag) in TikTok work like they do in Instagram.
- [ ] Instead of targeting broad audiences with hashtags like #fashion, go for fine targeting tags like #upcycledfashion or #streetstyle or #etsyfinds.
- [ ] Using two relevant hashtags in a post gets more engagement.
- [ ] Use this tool to learn which ones to apply: https://tiktokhashtags.com/

SELL ARTS & CRAFTS FROM UPCYCLED MATERIALS

> 🔊 **THE IMPACT OF REPURPOSING CLOTHING**
>
> Clothing is the #2 source of pollution globally (NERC.org). According to the New York Times, each American produces an average of 75 pounds of textile waste per year. Studies show reusing textiles is less harmful to the environment than recycling them. Close to four pounds of CO2 would be saved for every pound of clothing rescued from landfills (CO2List.org).

When you want to grow your side hustle into a larger business, selling to stores is the way to go. But it isn't for everyone. Keep reading to discover if building a wholesale operation is right for you.

> **MORE UPCYCLE PRODUCT IDEAS:**
>
> Brothers Matt and Jonny grew up loving the outdoors building dens and fashioning bows from natural materials. Now they use their crafting skills to make unique products from plastic waste. See their line of pens, coasters, pendants, combs, bowls, and other items at: https://www.brothersmake.com/. Check out their video content based on recycling at https://www.youtube.com/c/BrothersMake/featured. Their hope is to inspire others toward creative sustainability.

CHAPTER 18

Selling to Stores

Selling wholesale means selling to galleries and stores, who mark up the price and sell your upcycled art or crafts to their customers.

Wholesaling allows you to grow your business by getting stores and others to sell your pieces while you stay home and make them. The tips here will help you build relationships with one or as many store owners as you can handle.

Though the potential for scaling your side hustle upward through selling wholesale is huge, there is a price that comes with expansion. Growing a wholesale business can mean you will spend increasingly more of your time managing others and less time making products. This means training others. It means double-checking each item before shipping to make sure every piece was made with attention to details. It means calculating profit margins to the penny.

Here we look at what it means to get involved in selling to stores including:
- Preparing to sell wholesale
- Finding wholesale buyers
- Working with stores and galleries
- Overlooked retail outlets
- Selling one-of-a-kind pieces to galleries

PREPARING TO SELL WHOLESALE

Review Chapter 4 for tips on preparing your side hustle for growth. Some of the following tips appear there, too. They are important enough to repeat.

Know Your Profit Margin

In Chapter 5 on pricing, you learned how to determine your profit margin and whether you can sell your items wholesale.

Normally, if your production cost is one-fourth (or lower) of the store's retail price, you will make a profit. If a store's retail price is $25, your cost should be $6.25 or lower.

Stores typically mark an item's price at two and one-half times its cost. For example, if a store buys an item for $10, they will retail it for $25.

Production Capacity

How many items can you produce in one week? Is your production consistent and predictable? Stores and galleries like to show off new work. Can you envision coming up with fresh product ideas twice a year?

What Store Buyers Want

Be professional. Your business can be new, but should show signs you are serious about it. At the minimum, store buyers expect you to have a brand or business name, wholesale terms, catalog sheets of your work, and an artist's story.

It's also helpful to have a portfolio you can show them of your past work, previous gallery showings, and any media coverage you may have gotten.

When a store buyer asks your terms for wholesale accounts, here's an example to follow:

Jenny's Earth-Friendly Jewelry
Wholesale Terms

Net 30 terms available with approval upon your third order. Opening orders are prepaid via Visa, Mastercard, AmEx, Discover or PayPal or company check (with 7 business day delay.) Orders ship insured within 3 days via UPS or Priority Mail from Santa Fe, NM to addresses throughout US. Opening minimum order: $300, minimum reorder: $150. Prepaid orders of $250+ get free shipping to US addresses. Products are sold on a non-returnable basis. While rare, any defective merchandise may be returned at my expense within 14 days of delivery.

FINDING WHOLESALE BUYERS

There are several ways to locate stores and galleries:

<u>At art and craft shows, store buyers find you:</u> I have displayed my work at highly competitive art and craft shows, some attended by hundreds of thousands of shoppers. Store owners shop events looking for new products.

<u>Visit stores and galleries</u>: Walked by a store or gallery you would love to have your work in? Just go in and talk to the owner, unless the person is with a customer. In which case, quietly wait until they are free. Ask if you can make an appointment to show them your portfolio. If they aren't busy, they may want to look right then.

<u>LinkedIn.com</u>: Locate buyers online at the social network for business professionals. The following results showed up in searches made for people using the following phrases:
- 14,000 "accessories buyer"
- 2,200 "wearable art gallery"
- 9,500 "apparel buyer"
- 266,000 "interior designer"
- 5,900 "boutique owner"
- 7,400 "art buyer"
- 4,200 "bridal registry"

<u>Wholesale buying portals</u>. The websites below act as online portals where independent retail store buyers can purchase directly from makers. Each site has its own terms for listing products:

Tundra.com
Faire.com
Indieme.com
LAShowroom.com
Wholesaleinabox.com
Trouva.com (UK)

📢 PUBLICITY HELPS SECRETARY QUIT HER JOB

Jennifer Perkins got started as a kid making earrings from fishing lures which were sometimes covered in "slimy bait juice." As an adult, she created more sophisticated pieces she offered on her own website. *Bust Magazine* featured her handmade jewelry and site, resulting in a rush of orders. The write-up helped her quit her secretary job and expand sales into boutiques around the country. Source: Wall Street Journal

Working with Stores

When working with stores face-to-face, the checklist here will increase your success:

- [ ] Be on time for appointments. Don't show irritation if they are running late and need you to wait a bit.
- [ ] Have line sheets, price lists, product pages and business cards with you.
- [ ] Find an attractive bag or cases for carrying samples into stores. Cardboard boxes and garbage bags present a poor image.
- [ ] Show interest in the owner's store. They will appreciate compliments.
- [ ] Ask questions. Store buyers are usually happy to share advice to product makers. Ask them what their customers are buying this year, which colors are in, or how often they like to see new product lines.
- [ ] Not every store buyer you approach will buy. If you get a "no" be graceful and ask if the buyer has any suggestions about how to improve your work.
- [ ] Grow a rapport with your buyers and stay in touch. They carry many items from many makers. They could run out of one of your products and only remember to order when you check in to learn how they are doing.
- [ ] It is acceptable in wholesale to ask for payment at the time of a store buyer's first order; some makers ask for payment for the first two orders. After the initial purchase(s), be prepared to extend credit to your store account for 30 days. This is commonly called *net* 30.
- [ ] What if you have extended credit and the account does not pay? Remain calm. Avoid calling the store and angrily demanding payment. Remind them politely that you cannot ship more products until

they pay the outstanding invoices. If they haven't paid in ninety days, send a more strongly worded letter that asks for them to take care of the past due bills before you turn to a collection agency.

- [ ] If a buyer isn't pre-paying, ask for a purchase order number at the time they place an order. A purchase order is your proof that they placed an order.

- [ ] Stores usually pay shipping charges. Add this amount on to the invoice when billing.

- [ ] Encourage buyers to pay up front; offer free shipping when they pay at the time they order. This is big savings for them and many will jump on it. Know your profit margins and determine if you can afford to offer this perk.

- [ ] If you plan on doing craft shows in the same cities where you have store accounts, set your retail prices the same as the stores.

📣 **PLASTIC INTO MOSAIC PORTRAITS**

Lady Be transforms trashed plastic objects into mosaic tiles and then creates portraits of celebrities like Nelson Mandela, Paul McCartney, Marilyn Monroe and Audrey Hepburn. Her mission goes beyond creating art; she aims to help the fight against consumer waste, especially those involved in the plastics industry. Source: PlasticsNews.com.

Consignment

Consigning your products means that you leave your items at the store without receiving payment until sometime after the sale. The items remain your property until sold. Some makers don't like consignment. Others have a warmer attitude toward the arrangement.

Most galleries sell art on consignment. They get inventory on display at no cost to them. They also have the use of the money from the time of the sales untill the time they pay the artist, which is usually the month after the sale. Galleries split the sale 50/50, 60/40, or even 40/60 between the artisan and the shop.

Overlooked Retailers for Handmade Goods

Retail stores and boutiques aren't the only outlets for handmade products. Depending on what you make, check out these alternative markets:

- Businesses, organizations, and individuals hire interior designers to arrange their living or business spaces and find items to place there. Get your products in front of home and office interior buyers at houzz.com and artfulhome.com.
- Gift shops at airports, hotels, museums, hospitals, marinas carry handmade items. Locate gift shops at gift-shops.regionaldirectory.us
- Beauty salons and spas partner with jewelry and accessory makers. Find them at spaindex.com
- Campgrounds at national parks and tourist areas usually have gift shops. See reserveamerica.com/campgroundDirectory.do
- Fashion is going green. Check out boutiques for wearables. See elle.com/fashion/g8016/50-states-of-shopping-best-boutiques-in-america/
- Restaurants and cafes sometimes display art and crafts on their walls.
- Mail-order catalogs can be a market for your handmade products. One of the most popular for handmade items is the *Sundance Catalog*, started by Robert Redford. Neiman Marcus publishes a holiday catalog that showcases fine handcrafted items. The *Vermont Country Store* and *Coldwater Creek* catalog offers handmade interior accessories and gift ideas.

> 📣 **FASHIONABLE DRESSES MADE FROM TRASH**
>
> Like in most other areas of the world, Palestine faces its own growing trash problem. A younger generation of Palestinians are creatively repurposing old newspapers, bottle caps, candy wrappers, plastic bags and more into fashion-savvy dresses and accesories. Some make furniture and household decor items like lamps from discarded junk. Source: GulfNews.com.

Getting Your Upcycled Art in Galleries

There are many galleries and boutiques that represent one-of-a-kind work; and at much higher prices than gift stores. Most galleries work on consignment. Gallery owners will want to see a portfolio of your past and present work. You'll also want to have a professional looking "artist's story," personal photo, and top-notch images of your best work the gallery can have on hand to show interested clients. To find galleries, Google "gallery near me" or check out the directory at: art-collecting.com/galleries.htm

If making upcycled art is your thing, you will want to know about "art in public places" programs in many large cities. Winning a grant for public art can earn tens of thousands of dollars, free publicity, and keep you busy for some time. Keep reading to find these programs.

> **MORE UPCYCLE PRODUCT IDEAS:**
>
> CURA is a sustainable accessories brand using recycled plastic to create unique jewellery. Their philosophy revolves around 'reduce', 'reuse', 'recycle', and this philosophy extends to all parts of their business, from sourcing to manufacturing and packaging. Any waste, off-cuts, or parts deemed defective are recycled again and given new life. Check them out at: https://curajewellery.com/

CHAPTER 19

Upcycled Art in Public Art Programs

Feeling creative and want to make a big impression? Many states and larger cities sponsor "Percent for Art" or "Art in Public Places" programs.

These programs allocate funds toward the purchase and maintenance of public art as grants. Public art programs can be funded by government funds or as joint donations with private organizations contributing.

Public art programs award grants to artists whose applications and portfolios are reviewed and then selected by a jury. Because of the grant money and the value of the publicity, these programs are highly competitive.

A public art grant could bring an artist anywhere from $1,000 to a six-figure paycheck and loads of publicity. Millions of people may view the winning piece that could be displayed for a year or longer.

To learn if your city or community has a public art program, contact your city's arts council listed under "Arts Councils" or "Arts Agencies." Some public art money comes from large national grants disbursed to local arts agencies.

There are over 4,000 local and regional arts agencies around the U.S.. Many of these councils provide a variety of services that support arts and crafts in their communities including grants and funding arts in public places.

A way to find public art programs near you is to search online for *your city name* and "public art." To view examples of pieces that have been awarded public art grants, see publicartarchive.org.

> 📢 **$120,000 FOR PUBLIC ART**
>
> New Mexico's state flower, the yucca, became the inspiration for a recycled art in public places grant. Gordon Huether of California was the artist behind a 22'-high sculpture of a yucca plant, installed on the north side of I-40 driving into Albuquerque from the east. The $120,000+ piece was created from recycled fuel tanks. It was funded jointly among the city of Albuquerque, the state of New Mexico, and the US Department of Transportation.

Examples of Public Art Programs

US

Houston, TX, Public Art Program
houstontx.gov/culturalaffairs/civicartprogram.html

Los Angeles, CA, Public Arts
culturela.org/percent-public-art/public-works-improvements-arts-program-pwiap/

Miami, FL, Art in Public Places
miamidadepublicart.org

New York, NY, Percent for the Arts
nyc.gov/site/dclapercentforart/index.page

Phoenix, AZ, Arts Commission
phoenix.gov/arts/public-art-program

Tampa, FL, Public Art Program
tampagov.net/art-programs/Programs/public-art
Seattle, WA, Public Art Program
seattle.gov/arts/programs/public-art

CANADA

Montreal, CA, Public Art Program
artpublicmontreal.ca/en/

Toronto, CA, Public Arts
toronto.ca/explore-enjoy/history-art-culture/public-art/

Vancouver, CA, Public Arts
vancouver.ca/parks-recreation-culture/public-art.aspx

UK

London, UK, Public Art
cityoflondon.gov.uk/services/environment-and-planning/city-public-realm/Documents/city-arts-initiative-application-guidance-notes.pdf

AUSTRALIA

Sydney, AU
www.cityofsydney.nsw.gov.au/explore/arts-and-culture/public-art

GERMANY

Berlin, Germany
www.berlin.de/sen/kultur/en/funding/funding-programmes/public-art-and-percent-for-art/

No matter how you market your upcycled arts and crafts, your biggest asset is your list of customers. The next chapter describes ways to stay in touch with those people most likely to buy from you again.

CHAPTER 20

Your Customer List

Your customer mailing list is like gold. When you treat customers on your list with respect and generosity, they will reward you with their loyalty, their business, and their referrals.

A mailing list makes it easy to engage with people who have bought from you before. A study by the US Consumer Affairs Department says for every marketing dollar you spend to keep a current customer, you'll spend five dollars to get a new one.

Shoppers may never think of you after the first sale. One survey showed customers don't come back because:
- 3% relocated
- 5% were referred elsewhere by friends
- 9% succumbed to a competitor's better deal
- 14% became dissatisfied with their original purchase
- 68% were treated with indifference by an employee or business owner

The reason for most customer loss is also, by no coincidence, the category most often neglected by small business owners. Building a side hustle with staying power isn't just about making sales, it's about creating lasting relationships. This chapter explores ways to stay connected with your customers and coax them into lifetime loyalty. Learn the importance of:
- Capturing and working with e-mails
- Thirty-three excuses to follow up
- How to treat customers well

CAPTURING AND WORKING WITH E-MAILS

When you make a sale at a crafts fair or online, ask your customer if she would like to be on your mailing list. Many will say yes because they just found something from a seller they like. Take advantage of their enthusiasm. Even when a shopper shows interest but doesn't buy, the next best thing is to get them on your mailing list.

As mentioned earlier, when promoting on social media sites, capturing e-mail addresses should be one of your goals.

> 📣 **REBORN RESERVATION WRECKS**
>
> Native American Jay Laber Blackfeet crafted a bison from a Volkswagen Beetle, winning him the "People's Choice" award from the American Indian Higher Education Consortium. Another of his pieces, named "Charging Forward," is a statue of an iron Native American made from car parts mounted on an old Dodge Power Wagon. Jay specialized in blending Native American culture with mid-20th-century car parts scattered around the reservations. He called his studio 'Reborn Rez Wrecks.' He wanted his work to show how humans waste too much.

Apps for capturing and managing customer e-mails

The following apps help you capture e-mails and manage your mailing list. You can also create a series of autoresponders or send out a special offer or let your customers know about a new product you are launching: Aweber.com, Mailchimp.com, Getresponse.com, and Convertkit.com

These tools also allow you to personalize e-mails for better response. An example is an e-mail addressed to a person by first name in the e-mail subject area and with the person's name included in the body text of the e-mail. Personalized e-mails generate five times as many sales on average than non-personalized e-mails.

5 tips for e-mail:

- ☐ Improve your response rates by letting people know in the e-mail subject area and in the opening text of the e-mail the reason you are writing to them.
- ☐ People are busy, so get to the point of your message right away, whether it's letting them know about a special savings, a new product offer, or a craft show

you will be exhibiting at in their area.
- [ ] Remind customers who you are and your previous relationship with them.
- [ ] Send e-mail only to those people who have given you permission.
- [ ] When someone asks to be removed from your list, do it. Avoid getting pegged as a spammer. You can lose your account and face criminal charges if found to be in violation of the CanSpam Act.

THIRTY-THREE EXCUSES TO FOLLOW-UP

The average cost of getting new customers is six to ten times the cost of staying in touch with current ones. When you can't think of a good reason to reconnect with your contacts, here are thirty-three excuses to reach out and remind people of you.

- [ ] Thank someone for visiting your booth at an event
- [ ] Thank your customer after each sale
- [ ] Thank someone for their time, even if they didn't buy
- [ ] Announce a special sale
- [ ] Announce a contest
- [ ] Announce a new product release
- [ ] Announce a limited-edition series
- [ ] Send a product sample
- [ ] Advise about discontinued items
- [ ] Send a gift
- [ ] Learn if a customer got their order
- [ ] Learn if a customer got your letter, flyer, or communication
- [ ] Send a newsletter
- [ ] Send a postcard or flyer with a schedule of your upcoming shows and exhibits

- [ ] Send a product tip sheet
- [ ] Send a product catalog
- [ ] Ask for a referral
- [ ] Thank someone for a referral
- [ ] Invite high-dollar customers to dinner as a way of expressing appreciation
- [ ] Offer a coupon or incentive to get customers to come back
- [ ] Offer to link to someone's website from your own
- [ ] Make your customer feel important by creating a preferred customer offering
- [ ] Send a news clipping or copy of an article appearing about you
- [ ] Share ideas for holiday gifts and special occasions
- [ ] Send interesting facts about the piece a customer bought
- [ ] Seek a host for a home party or trunk show
- [ ] Thank someone for sponsoring a home party or trunk show
- [ ] Send a customer survey asking for feedback on how you measured up for service and quality of product
- [ ] Encourage more orders by sending testimonials from satisfied customers
- [ ] Send cards celebrating holidays other than Christmas—like Mother's Day, Graduation, Thanksgiving, and Valentine's Day
- [ ] Resolve a conflict or problem the customer had
- [ ] Make amends for a mistake you made
- [ ] Link your fiber craft products to one of the specially recognized months. As mentioned earlier, January is special because it is: Chilly Month,

National Eye Care Month, National Soup Month, Whale-Watching Month, National Egg Month, National Wheat Bread Month, and much more.

Using a daily planner, make a follow-up calendar scheduling the above action steps so you don't forget them.

TREAT CUSTOMERS WELL

Customers talk to their friends about their shopping experiences, especially when they feel they've been treated badly. On average, an unhappy customer tells from seven to fifteen others about their negative experience.

Customers are more likely to leave a negative review when they have a bad experience than take time to write a positive review. Since reviews are the fuel for online sales, make it a priority to fix customer issues immediately to avoid getting bad reviews.

Customers are five times more likely to stop doing business with someone because of mistreatment than because of any other reason.

Building and maintaining your customer list is one of many important practices covered in this book.

If you have made it this far without feeling overwhelmed, you are doing great! If you feel confused about what to do first, keep in mind, you don't have to do everything at the same time. Take baby steps. You'll get where you want to go.

Focusing on key fundamentals will help you reach your aim faster, cheaper, and with more joy. Make your priorities the elements found in the *Success Pattern*.

CHAPTER 21

The Success Pattern

I've sold my handmade crafts in a variety of markets for over thirty years. My last side hustle brought in over $134,000 from craft shows, selling online, and wholesaling to stores. I got there following the steps outlined in this guide. From my experiences, a *Success Pattern* emerged of what works and what doesn't in promoting handmade items.

> *Government regulations require that I add a disclaimer here that my statement of earnings does not guarantee or promise you will achieve similar or any results following my recommendations.*

The parts we covered in this book that most influence the *Success Pattern* include:
- your love or enthusiasm for what you do
- your personal story
- the colors and quality of your product design
- your images
- your packaging
- your displays
- your profit margins
- your marketing plan

Separately, they each play an important role. Together, they combine into a dynamic synergy. As you fine-tune the elements, they affect each other and become more than the sum of the parts. They bring you to *creative control* of your side gig and your life. It's a sweet place to be!

When you continually improve the fundamentals above, your products will stand out from others, your sales will increase, and you will feel empowered.

As much as I would love to, I can't promise success in your side hustle. So much depends on your inner game: how you look at life, whether you see opportunities everywhere, or see yourself a victim of your circumstances.

I've been in both places and I know how challenging staying positive can be. Thinking positive and having an unshakable belief in yourself are the keys to making everything in this book work for you.

I hope you will use those keys to open the doors of opportunity. I've shown you where the doors are. Now go and unlock them. I celebrate your journey to success!

Appendices

Appendix 1

Product Photography

Great photos convert online shoppers into buyers. If you are just starting to gather images or you want to uplevel from what you have been using, look to the images used on successful Etsy shops (EtsyRank.com) and note how their pics are sharp and clear, well-lit, and show off the product from a variety of angles.

There are six types of product images that help sell your products:

1. **Product-only images with white background** for online store listings. Studies show the white background improves online sales. White background images are required when selling on Amazon, but not on Etsy.

2. **How-it's-made images**. Pictures of you making your products. Shoppers like to see artisans at work. Tell your "how I made this" story through photos.

3. **Step-by-step instructional images** where a person in the photo shows how to use a product, if applicable. My sales doubled when I started including a "how to wear" card with every purchase. The card showed nine different ways to wear the item.

4. **Lifestyle images** showing people in real-life poses enjoying your item. If you can get them, use images of real customers (who have given permission) using your products. You can also use models (found several on Fiverr as mentioned below) using your item.

5. **Jury images** to submit when applying to arts and crafts fairs. While I'm writing this, many craft shows have canceled due to Covid, but hopefully shows and events will return as a marketing venue.

6. **Head shots** of you to accompany your artist's story in your promotional materials and your social media profiles.

DIY Photography Tips

The images you use in your listings may be the single most important influence on converting visitors to buyers. The following tactics will help your images sell for you:

• When selling 3-dimensional objects, include photos taken from different viewpoints so viewers get a sense of depth. Each view should be looking straight at the object. Angle shots make an item look skewed or damaged.

• Take photos in daylight or under Halogen lights (whiter light) or color-balanced lighting.

• Your image colors should be bright with good contrast between dark and lighter areas.

• Digital images can be cropped, color-balanced, contrasted, and enhanced in many ways using a photo-management app.

• For previewing your images, set your own monitor at the highest color resolution. But be aware most computer monitors will view colors slightly different. Older monitors show less accurate color resolution.

• Copying other people's images from Web sites, auctions or print publications is illegal. Unless you see a notice or have evidence that an image is in the Public Domain, assume that every image you see is copyright protected.

If you are on a tight budget or you just want to do your own photography, the following sites offer tutorials:
- alison.com/tag/photography
- youtube.com/user/tutvid/playlists
- bit.ly/PHLearnVids (Photoshop tutorials)

Finding photographers

Commercial product photographers can cost hundreds of dollars. When you engage a professional, you quickly learn they charge additional fees for copyrights as well as the photos themselves. Though you get great pics, you may not have the funds to invest so much money starting out. Cheaper alternatives:

At Fiverr.com I searched for "product photography" and found affordable rates. Copyright is included in the fees. Look for providers with positive reviews and many completed gigs. I only work with those who have received multiple five-star ratings.

Another source for finding photographers is Etsy.com. Type in the search bar: "product photography" for thousands of results. Most services are for product images only, not models. If your product needs a model, expect to pay more.

Also search for "mockup" on Etsy for thousands of examples of products in lifestyle settings.

CreativeMarket.com and DesignCuts.com offer a huge collection of mockups for simulating your product image in a lifestyle setting.

For more craft photography tips, see the book, *Photographing Arts, Crafts & Collectibles* by Steve Meltzer.

APPENDIX 2

Find Events

Art and Craft Shows, Festivals, Expos

Find events to display your upcycled crafts according to your location. The more competitive (popular and well-attended) events have cut-off dates, so apply early.

US & Canada

- zapplication.org
- art-linx.com
- artfaircalendar.com
- festivalnet.com

UK

- craftyfoxmarket.co.uk
- handmadeinbritain.co.uk
- designersmakers.com
- 10times.com/london-uk/arts-crafts
- UKcraftfairs.com
- artfaircalendar.com
- prima.co.uk/leisure/events/a39073/best-craft-festivals-in-the-uk/
- renegadecraft.com/city/london

Europe

- artfaircalendar.com/art_fair/european-eu-uk-germany-france-art-shows.html
- Across Europe, open-air markets centrally located to attract tourist traffic are almost everywhere, even in smaller cities.

Australia

- craftevents.com.au

- expertiseevents.com.au
- artfaircalendar.com
- sydneycraftweek.com

India and Asia

- artfaircalendar.com/art_fair/asia-japan-hong-kong-korea-art-fairs.html
- Open-air markets are in most cities, as in Europe.

International

- makerfaire.com

APPENDIX 3

Where to List Online
Around the World

Etsy accepts payments from many countries aruond the world. Amazon Handmade also allows sellers to reach international customers.

US & Canada

- etsy.com
- amazon.com/Handmade/
- zibbet.com
- bonanza.com
- artfulhome.com
- ecrater.com
- houzz.com
- makersmarket.us
- patreon.com
- uncommongoods.com
- icraftgifts.com (Canada based)
- latitudesdecor.com

UK

- thefuturekept.com
- folksy.com
- madebyhandonline.com
- misi.co.uk
- miratis.com
- designersmakers.com
- designnation.co.uk
- aerende.co.uk
- personalise.co.uk
- thecraftersbarn.co.uk
- notonthehighstreet.com
- rebelsmarket.com

- artsthread.com
- affordablebritishart.co.uk
- art2arts.co.uk
- artpistol.co.uk
- artclickireland.com
- creativeboom.com

Europe

- riotart.co
- artbaazar.com
- artebooking.com
- zet.gallery

Australia

- madeit.com.au
- stateoftheartgallery.com.au
- artloversaustralia.com.au
- artpharmacy.com.au

India and Asia

- melaartisans.com
- artisera.com
- artzyme.com

International

- artsyshark.com/sell-art-online-directory/
- eclecticartisans.com (handmade jewelry)
- Facebook Marketplace is available to people over 18 in the US, UK, Australia, New Zealand and Mexico on the Facebook app

APPENDIX 4

Recycled Art Contests

Another way to earn cash, get publicity, and build reputation is through winning recycled art contests.

Ripley's *Believe it or Not* sponsored *Ripcycle, Unbelievable Art Contest*. The first place went to artist Rob Surette and earned him $2,000. His portrait of Taylor Swift assembled from over 17,000 gum balls became a part of the famous Ripley's Collection.

ReStore is a brick and mortar supplier of used construction material whose proceeds go to Habitat for Humanity. ReStore sponsors an *Annual Recycled Art Contest* in their Milwaukee location. The contest encourages artworks made primarily from donated items found at ReStore. The public votes for the winners—first prize takes home $250.

In San Carlos, CA, a *Trash-to-Art Contest* encourages students to create and submit an art piece using materials destined for landfills. Mediums include sculptures, collages and murals. Winners get recognition and their pieces go on display at the local Shoreway Environmental Education Center.

The Maryland Department of the Environment (MDE) in Baltimore sponsors an annual *Rethink Recycling* sculpture contest for high school students. Winners receive national recognition, TV news airtime, and prizes provided by sponsors. More and more school programs are encouraging students to get creative with recycling.

To find programs near you, search for "recycled art contests" for locally sponsored competitions.

About the Author

James Dillehay is an artisan, former gallery owner, and author of twelve books. He has sold his handmade products at some of the top juried shows in the US, in galleries and boutiques from Manhattan to the Grand Canyon, and online at Etsy, Ebay, and Amazon.

James developed and presented crafts marketing programs for the University of Alaska, Northern New Mexico Community College, Bootcamp for Artists and Craftspeople, and The Learning Annex.

He currently lives, writes, and creates cool stuff from a studio he built (and it doesn't leak) next to a national forest in New Mexico.

See hundreds of ideas for recycled and upcycled art and crafts on James' Pinterest board at: **https://www.pinterest.com/JamesDillehay/repurposed-crafts/**.

Resources

Access the resources and downloads described in this book at: **Craftmarketer.com/book-resources/**

FREE Bonus

Free Ebook Reveals Blueprint Used by Top Sellers to Boost Sales + Profits

Looking for a *blueprint for selling your handmade products*? I wish I had one back in those early years of struggling with unknowns, false starts, and misdirections.

What if you could bypass those startup pains and grow your sales and profits, faster and easier? Now, you can with the ***Blueprint for Selling Handmade Products*** ebook.

It outlines **proven tips** from over twenty years of selling handmade items in multiple markets.

Download this gift from the author. Get your **free** ebook (PDF) now at: **Craftmarketer.com/bp/**

Made in United States
North Haven, CT
20 March 2024